# AN OUTDOOR KITCHEN
# FULL OF SUNSHINE

by

Kris Mazy

Copyright © 2014 Kris Mazy
www.MazyBooks.com
Chino Valley, AZ
All rights reserved.

ISBN-13: 978-1479112302
ISBN-10: 1479112305

# DEDICATION

This book is dedicated to

All of my "Littles" –


Rowan, Berlyn, Breckin and Trystan

And solar cooking so that we can spend more

time together as a family

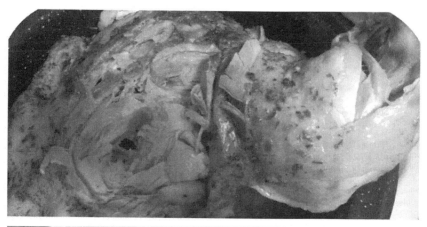

# INTRODUCTION

As any parent, I find ways to save money in my budget and to spend more time with my children. Larry and I now have 7 children. We added 2 additions through adoption in 2013 to our already fantastic clan of munchkins.

How does a mom of 7 spend more time with her family and save a few dollars in the process? Solar cooking has been my answer. We have gone "back to the basics" and allowed ourselves to be better parents in the process. When we first started this journey of learning how to solar oven cook in our household, I had no idea that we could make so many delicious foods in a solar oven. Heck, until 4 years ago, I had no idea that people used solar ovens to cook their foods!

My very first dish was a cheese stuffed meatloaf. That has become a staple meal in our home. We have since altered our recipe to fit the ever-changing family needs and now use gluten-free bread crumbs.

Using a solar oven, I have the opportunity to put "dinner in the oven" in the morning and spend more time playing outdoors with my kids. I am never worried that my oven is on and am comfortable leaving the house while dinner is cooking.

With solar cooking, I use the sun as my energy to cook everything from bread to desserts, from main dishes to sides and everything in between. I keep my house cool in the summer time, and in Arizona, that is a good thing. We are saving on our propane for inside cooking, saving on energy costs for our cooler and keeping the house a normal temperature. Our power bill is high enough as it is, so this is something that is important to us by keeping that bill down.

This means that my inside stove and oven don't get turned on and we only use the outside for all of our cooking needs. On average we use our solar oven at least 3-4 times a week. Most of the other days, we BBQ!

Since 2011, our family has been creating, testing and well, of course, eating meals out of our solar oven.

My sister, Jen, uses her solar oven often and so do my parents. Once we began talking to friends in our community, we discovered that there are many people who also use solar ovens as well.

We also found that there is not a lot of literature out there on how to use a solar oven and what your can make in it. We have discovered a whole new world of cooking for our family and are constantly adding new recipes to our list. This doesn't mean that every attempt has turned out, but we have had fun none the less. This cookbook is a result of all of our family notes, tried and true recipes. – ONLY the goods are in here. I promise that I didn't put any of the failed attempts!!

There have been days that I have gotten food into my oven and didn't have enough time – This will mostly happen in the summer when we have monsoon season here in Arizona and I don't get "dinner in the oven" by about 8 am and the monsoon rains begin just after lunch. Great for the plants and temperature! Bad for my dinner in my solar oven! Those days, I needed to bake it for an extra 30 minutes in the oven at home. Many days, we prep all of our dinner foods the night before in order to get them out and in the oven by 8am. Then, it is a worry-free day!

When we are camping, I always prepare our meal right after breakfast and often time I have it pre-prepared in a zipper bag to just throw in the oven to make the camp trip even simpler.

Each child in our family has a favorite and a specialty that they like to help create from the solar oven. We marked them in this book, with their name. With having 7 children with individual tastes, you can bet that they argue over what we are making for dinner.

One of our sons, Berlyn, hates trying new things. He is autistic and routine is so very important to him. One night, we attempted to try stuffed chicken with a side of cheesy turnips and radishes. He argued for an hour that the salad could not be on the inside of the chicken. Once he tasted it with the melted parmesan cheese and cooked spinach he asked for it for the next 3 nights. We actually had to attempt this dish 3 times before we even got to eat it, thanks to our 3 black labs, Robbie, Hunter, and Scouty.

In 2013, Larry and I adopted 2 amazing little boys through Arizona Foster Care. Trystan, our youngest is gluten and lactose intolerant. Our little boys, because of their abuse and neglect, are always fascinated with the solar oven (actually with cooking and eating food in general) and I can often find them checking the temperature of it through the days when they are home.

Our middle daughter, Elwyn is anaphylactic to red dyes. It makes eating many foods quite "interesting" in our home with multiple kids on restricted diets. We have relearned how to cook over and over again. And don't buy processed foods.

We have altered our eating over the years to accommodate our ever changing family. We cook everything from scratch. We buy most foods in bulk and have a huge garden every year. We can and process foods so that we can eat them throughout the year. We also dehydrate many fruits and other foods to make a variety of different snacks for the kids. During the summer time, we often eat in a semi-paleo diet where we eliminate all grains and go for a mostly meat and veggie diet.

We have converted many of our recipes to "Gluten-Free" and everything in this book is dye-free as long as if you don't pick up processed items such as tomato sauce without checking. In the process, we have added a gluten-free symbol to all of the recipes that we know are gluten-free. (Thank you Rhiannon for helping me on this gluten-free journey for my son!) Most of them can be converted as well. For instance, changing the teriyaki sauce to a gluten-free version, which is what we use alters the recipe to make it safe for my son, Trystan, to eat.

# GLUTEN FREE

This book originally did not start off as a gluten-free book. It has turned into that as we are continually watching what we eat with our kids and altering our own recipes.

Watch for the Gluten Free Symbol for those recipes that are written as gluten free.

Most recipes in this book that are not marked as GF can be altered to fit a gluten free lifestyle as well.

# WHAT IS GLUTEN-FREE AND WHY DO WE EAT THAT WAY IN OUR HOUSE?

When we started this gluten-free journey, we had NO IDEA what we were getting into! Our 6 year old son Trystan was adopted through Arizona Foster Care in May of 2013. He came into our home as a foster child in July of 2012 along with his brother, Breckin.

From July 2012 until May 2013, Trystan always had focus issues and tummy problems. We tried everything under the sun to get him to feel better. The week after his adoption at the end of May, 2013, I had taken him back to the doctor for the tenth time about his tummy issues.

Our doctor suggested that for the summer, we try to go paleo and eliminate dairy and grains from our diet to see if that would help. Trystan's blood work came back as minor dairy allergies and negative for celiac (which is a much larger problem – and we are so thankful that it wasn't worse.) Less than 2 weeks after changing his diet he felt better.

We knew what the problem was... Now, it was up to me to discover how we could change our diet to eat better! And I had to relearn how to cook and bake all over again! This was after discovering Elwyn's severe red dye allergy in 2005 and after our first cookbook, *A Kitchen Full of Mixes.*

Gluten is the protein that initially makes bread elastic and rise. It is found in mainly wheat, rye and barley, but there are other grains that contain it too. Like dyes, it is found in so many different items that you can pick up in the "middle aisles" (processed food isles) of the grocery store. We are thankful that there are now more and more stores out there that are becoming more conscious of healthier eating and that type of lifestyle. We have 5+ store within 30 miles of our home that carries natural, organic and gluten-free.

Gluten-free is not for everyone. I still bake bread 2 times a week because I can't be without my cheesy dinner artisan bread.

For Trystan, it affects his intestines with processing food, causes a "tick" and brain fog.  There have been so many times that we have gotten calls from his school or other activities where they notice a "strange change" in him suddenly. His intolerance is so bad that we have decided to home school him with some of our other kids so that we can take the gluten factor out of his reach.

I will always remember the day about a week after beginning a gluten-free journey with him when he was extremely animated and drug me into the bathroom to show me what he "left" in the potty! Seriously, EEWWW! I was healing his insides and we were all eating better in the process.

# BASIC MEASUREMENTS

| Unit: | Equals: | Also equals: |
|---|---|---|
| 1 teaspoon. | 1/6 fl. oz. | 1/3 Tablespoon. |
| 1 Tablespoon. | ½ fl. oz. | 3 teaspoon. |
| 1/8 cup | 1 fl. oz. | 2 Tablespoon. |
| ¼ cup | 2 fl. oz. | 4 Tablespoon. |
| 1/3 cup | 2¾ fl. oz. | ¼ cup plus 4 teaspoon. |
| ½ cup | 4 fl. oz. | 8 Tablespoon. |
| 1 cup | 8 fl. oz. | ½ pint |
| 1 pint | 16 fl. oz. | 2 cups |
| 1 quart | 32 fl. oz. | 2 pints |
| 1 liter | 34 fl. oz. | 1 quart plus ¼ cup |
| 1 gallon | 128 fl. oz. | 4 quarts |

# CONTENTS

# ACKNOWLEDGMENTS

Thank you God for my faith
and Your guidance in my life.

Thank you to my husband, Larry Fullmer for his willing
to help test all of my recipes over the last 17 years.

Thank you to my parents, Jan and Dave Mazy for
believing that I could create this and my other cookbooks
and for their support in this endeavor with testing, tasting
and proofing recipes for me.

Thank you to my sister, Jen and her husband, Jason
(plus the boys) for helping out in every way that they can in
all parts of our lives.

Thank you to all of my children for eating everything
that I cook. (And most of the time with no complaints!)

And lastly, THANK YOU to all of my friends who are
gluten-free and paleo eating! You have helped me
immensely over the last 2 years (Linda, my sis Jen,
Rhiannon and so many others who have answered my bug-
zillion questions about gluten-free as I started
experimenting with different foods and flours)!!

# LET'S GET STARTED!
## WHAT IS SOLAR OVEN COOKING?

Here are the basics to Solar Oven cooking:

1.    Solar oven cooking uses the sun's natural energy to cook your food.

2.    Solar cooking saves money by saving on your energy bills whether electricity or propane etc.  After your initial investment in either purchasing an oven (see page 5) or building your own (see page 175), there are no other investments besides your cost of food.

3.    Solar ovens are safe to use even for families with children.  (Although, if you have 3 black labs, you need to watch where you put your oven, because they LOVE spinach stuffed chicken and have knocked over my oven not once, but twice to get to those cheesy stuffed yummies!)

4.    You can cook virtually ANYTHING in a solar oven – for one person or for many people – Think about it! We cook for at least 9 people at any given meal! This is practically a sunshine crockpot.

5.    Your kitchen will not be heated up in the summer time so you are not running your cool air because of cooking.

# WHAT CAN YOU COOK IN YOUR SOLAR OVEN?

You can cook anything that you can create in your crockpot or in your oven. You can cook anything from casseroles to pot roast. And with the correct sunny day, you can even cook bread and cookies. The solar oven will never get "hot" enough to fry anything however, so keep that in mind. The solar oven will not "brown" your bread.

I will however not recommend cooking broccoli in your oven as it makes the inside of the oven smell horrible. (I speak from experience.) We don't bake fish in it terrible often because of the smell as well; however it isn't as bad as broccoli. Pasta doesn't always fair too well either (We have added 2 recipes with pasta, but know that they will NOT have the same texture as what you would get boiling it in the house. They become more of a gooey layer that you have to adjust your palate to enjoy. )

My oldest son, Griffen is one to experiment with foods often. I am always getting asked if "this" herb would taste good on "this" meat. I am always looking forward to having Griffen in the kitchen because I know that he will throw something tasty together.

# WHEN CAN I USE MY SOLAR OVEN?

You can use your solar on days that have at least 20 minutes of sun every 60 minutes and at least 5 hours of cook time. The strongest time to cook is between 10 am and 2pm. Temperatures inside your oven need to reach over 180 degrees to cook the food. Reflectors can be used to help get that temperature higher in your oven. I use my reflectors year round, but my sister doesn't use her oven in the summertime here in Arizona. My reflectors have been altered over the years because of constant use and I saw that they were repaired with Christmas ribbon this week. Only in my house!

Many people have used the solar ovens in northern locations (northern US and into Canada.) All you need is to make sure that the oven is pointing towards the sun throughout the day and that the temperature with the reflectors gets up to over 180 degrees. If you are cooking something that needs 6-8 hours to complete, in the winter times, you may need to turn your oven slightly throughout the day to make sure that it is getting full sunlight to keep the temperature.

We do take our solar oven in our RV when we travel and use often while camping to ease the chaoticness of cooking for 9 over a campfire.

# WHERE CAN I GET A SOLAR OVEN?

You can either make your own or purchase one. Our online family shop carries the one that I and out family all uses in stock because they have become so popular - **www.Mazys.com**. There are many different types of solar ovens. We carry ones from the Solar Oven Society.

Page 175 of this book has directions on making a very simple solar oven. My boys are constantly "adjusting" their designs on their homemade ovens at our house. I mainly use the one from S.O.S. that we carry in the shop.

## www.Mazys.com

Our oven sets include an oven with lid, 2 pots with lids, thermometer, reflectors, WAPI (water pasteurization indicator) and instruction manual.

These ovens are so east to set up, I often find my 10-year old, El, prepping for our dinner meal!

# TIPS IN USING THE SOLAR OVEN

- Dark pots work better that light pots.
- Short or shallow pots work better that tall ones.
- Several small pots work better than one large one.
- Food cooks faster when there is a lid on the pot.
- There is no need to add water to your dishes unless the recipe calls for it, like cooking beans.
- More water = more cook time.
- Cutting food into smaller pieces allows food to cook faster.
- The more the food in the oven, the longer that it will take to cook.
- Don't expect bread to brown and crisp or pasta to cook the same as inside the house.

# USING OUR OVENS WHILE CAMPING

## A family story

Going on our full family camping trips is so much fun in our family.   With 16+ people in attendance and many times friends go with us as well we take enough games and supplies for all of the kids. We are never short on activities or on food. My parents, sister and her family and mine all go on an annual campout often times up to Williams, Arizona, up in the mountains where the air is thin and there are more pine trees that you can count.

I am sure that it is quite a sight seeing all 3 of our solar oven lined up by our tents and RVs each day. We eat like kings while camping by taking our ovens with us and can manage 3 or 4 different dishes at each evening meal. And no one ever goes away hungry when camping with us!

While camping, if we are at a camp ground, we often have people come up to use and ask questions about what we are cooking and how. It is quite the conversational piece. We will ask people to join us too for dinner at camp grounds. Solar ovens cook a lot more than basic camping food.

# GETTING STARTED

Here are some fast and easy "starter" recipes that you can get to know your solar oven and learn how to cook with it.

- Heating Hot Dogs
- Cheesy Garlic Bread
- Pita Pizzas
- Nachos
- Party Mix
- Granola

These recipes are the bare minimums that your oven can do. You can use it for basic "heating" up of food. This chapter will help guide you with a few "getting started" recipes.

I told my kids NO COOKING in the kitchen while mom was gone one day when I needed to run out of the house. I came home to a handful of mini-pizzas, piping hot. Asking Elwyn what she did, I got an eye roll from my 10 year old daughter. She replied simply with "mom you said no cooking IN the kitchen."

# Heating up Hot Dogs Or Sausages

This is a fast and easy lunch when you go to the park or on a camping trip. This will heat up your hot dogs while you are out throwing a baseball or Frisbee!

Ingredients:

- 1 package of hot dogs or Italian sausages

Directions:
1. Set up solar oven.
2. Add hot dogs to solar oven pan.
3. Add pan with lid to solar oven and seal.
4. Let cook for 90 minutes in oven or until hot dogs are heated through. On a really sunny warm day, this could take less than an hour.

Heat a can of chili in the other solar oven pan to create chili dogs! A favorite in our house!

Serve on buns or rolls with your favorite toppings.

# Cheesy Garlic Bread

## INGREDIENTS:

- I loaf of sour dough bread
- 1 stick of butter, soft
- 4 cloves of garlic, pressed or minced
- 1/2 cup of grated cheese (cheddar, mozzarella, or colby jack)
- Aluminum foil

## DIRECTIONS:

1. Set up solar oven.
2. Slice bread long ways from end to end.
3. In small bowl, stir together butter and garlic.
4. Spread butter mixture on inside of each half.
5. Lay bottom half on plate.
6. Spread cheese on bottom half and place top half back on bread to form a compete loaf.
7. Wrap aluminum foil all the way around the bread and wrap ends up so that there is no leaking in your oven.
8. Put wrapped bread in bottom of solar oven and seal oven.
9. Let heat for 1 hour in oven or until cheese melts.

# Pita Pizzas

## INGREDIENTS:

- 2 pita breads
- 4 Tablespoons red sauce
- 1/2 cup grated cheese
- 1/4 cup pepperoni
- 1 teaspoon Italian seasoning – page 186

## DIRECTIONS:

1. Set up solar oven.
2. In solar oven, place solar oven pans upside down to make a flat and open cooking area.
3. On a cutting board, lay a pita flat.
4. Add 2 Tablespoons of sauce, half of the pepperoni and half of the cheese.
5. Sprinkle with Italian seasoning.
6. Place pizza on the upside down pan in the oven
7. Repeat with second pita and again add to solar oven.
8. Seal oven and let heat for 30 minutes or until cheese is melted

# Nachos

## INGREDIENTS:

- Corn tortilla chips
- 1 can of refried beans
- 1 cup of cheddar cheese, grated
- 1-4 ounce can of green chilies
- 1-4 ounce can of olives, chopped
- 3 green onions, sliced thin

Topped with guacamole (page 58), sour cream and salsa

## DIRECTIONS:

1. Set up solar oven.
2. Layer chips in solar oven pans, evenly.
3. Follow with beans, cheese, chilies, olives and green onions, divided equally between both solar oven pans. Layer each ingredient in pan.
4. Add pans with lids to solar oven and seal.
5. Let cook for 1 hour in oven or until beans are heated through.

# Party Mix

INGREDIENTS:

- 3 cups Corn Chex™ or Rice Chex™ cereal (love that this cereal is gluten free!)
- 1/2 cup dry-roasted peanuts
- 1 tablespoon olive oil
- 2 tablespoons grated Parmesan cheese
- 1/2 teaspoon chili powder – page 90
- 1/2 teaspoon garlic powder

DIRECTIONS:

1. Set up solar oven.
2. In a separate bowl, mix together all ingredients. Mix well.
3. Pour into solar oven pan.
4. Add pan with lid to solar oven and seal.
5. Let cook for 1 hour in oven

# Granola

## INGREDIENTS:

- 1/3 cup coconut oil or 1/3 cup butter, melted
- 1/3 cup honey
- 1/4 cup brown sugar
- 1 teaspoon vanilla
- 1/2 teaspoons cinnamon
- 1/4 teaspoon nutmeg
- 2-1/2 cups old fashioned oats (not quick oats)
- Optional: almond slivers or chopped almonds
- Optional: dried fruits and shredded coconut

We often double this recipe and it disappears as quickly as we make it.

## DIRECTIONS:

1. Set up solar oven.
2. In a separate bowl, mix together all ingredients. Mix well.
3. Grease sides and bottom of solar oven pan. (The honey in this recipe makes this mixture a bit sticky.)
4. Pour into solar oven pan.
5. Add pan with lid to solar oven and seal.
6. Let cook for 90 minutes in oven.

After you remove the granola, dump pan contents on a sheet of parchment or wax paper and let cool. This will help with clean-up and prevent the granola from sticking to the pan.

# Add your Own Getting Started Dish

Title: _____

INGREDIENTS:

| | |
|---|---|
| _____ | _____ |
| _____ | _____ |
| _____ | _____ |
| _____ | _____ |
| _____ | _____ |
| _____ | _____ |

DIRECTIONS:

_____

_____

_____

_____

_____

_____

_____

_____

_____

_____

_____

_____

_____

# Add your Own Getting Started Dish

Title: _____

## INGREDIENTS:

_____    _____

_____    _____

_____    _____

_____    _____

_____    _____

_____    _____

_____    _____

## DIRECTIONS:

_____

_____

_____

_____

_____

_____

_____

_____

_____

_____

_____

_____

# Add your Own Getting Started Dish

Title: _____

INGREDIENTS:

_____    _____
_____    _____
_____    _____
_____    _____
_____    _____
_____    _____

DIRECTIONS:

_____
_____
_____
_____
_____
_____
_____
_____
_____
_____
_____
_____

# MEAT DISHES

- Basic Chicken Breasts
- Whole Chicken
- Chicken and Mushrooms
  - Gluten-free Cream of Mushroom Soup (Stove-top extra recipe)
- Jen's Easy Solar Oven Chicken Meal
- Cilantro Lime Chicken
- Honey Mustard Chicken
- Cubed Chicken with Green Chilies
- Spinach Stuffed Chicken Breasts
- Roast with Dried Tomatoes
- Pineapple Chicken
- Mediterranean Beef
- Meat Loaf
- Brown Sugar Ham
- Stuffed Bell Peppers
- Apples & Pork
- Jalapenos Cream Cheese Chicken
- Beef Fajita
  - Guacamole
- Pulled Pork (or Chicken)
  - Homemade BBQ Sauce (Stove-top extra recipe)
- Wrapped Tilapia
- Dill Lemon While Fish
- Bleu Cheese Steak Roll-ups
- Chicken Cordon Bleu Roll-up
- Hobo Stew
- Kielbasa Veggie Bake

# Basic Chicken Breasts

## INGREDIENTS:

- 4 chicken breasts

## OPTIONAL SEASONINGS:

- Lemon Pepper (We mix our own seasonings so that we know EXACTLY what we are eating There is so much added salt in many of the prepackaged seasonings that we try and avoid what we can. See Page 187 for our Lemon Pepper Recipe)
- Italian Seasoning (We make our own from our herbs in our garden. – See Page 186 For our recipe)
- Onion Mix – Page 188
- Salt and Pepper to taste
- 1 Tablespoon olive oil or coconut oil
- Basil or pesto sauce

You can season your chicken with any herb or combination of herbs and spices that you would normally do in the oven.

Many times when I am cooking chicken, I will cook enough meat for 2 different meals.

Then, I use the 2nd day for recipes like my enchiladas or soft tacos by adding beans and tomatoes, alfredo chicken with white sauce over pasta or even on top of fresh green salads to make a chicken salad. It makes dinner even easier for the next night.

DIRECTIONS:

1. Set up solar oven.
2. Rinse chicken and add to solar oven pan.
3. Season to taste.
4. Add pan with lid to solar oven and seal.
5. Let cook for 6-8 hours in oven or until it is no longer pink.

Note: the larger the chicken, the longer that it will take to cook.

# Whole Chicken

## INGREDIENTS:

- 1 whole chicken

## OPTIONAL SEASONINGS:

- Lemon Pepper –
  page 187
- Italian Seasoning –
  page 186
- Onion Mix – Page
  188
- Salt and Pepper to
  taste
- 1 Tablespoon olive
  oil or coconut oil
- Basil or pesto sauce

Did you know that a whole chicken can fit into one of the solar oven pans?

We wait until whole chickens go on sale at the local market and stock up!

## DIRECTIONS:

1. Set up solar oven.
2. Rinse chicken (Don't forget to check the chicken for the gizzards!) and add to solar oven pan.
3. Season to taste.
4. Add pan with lid to solar oven and seal.
5. Let cook for 6-8 hours in oven or until it is no longer pink.

This cooked chicken can be used for ANY dish that calls for chicken. You can make chicken tacos, add it to salads, add the meat in lasagna or just pull it off of the bone and eat it straight.

# Chicken and Mushrooms

INGREDIENTS:

- 4 chicken breasts
- 1 16oz package of fresh Mushrooms, washed and sliced
- 1 Tablespoons Italian seasonings, page 186
- 1/2 teaspoon salt
- 1/2 teaspoon pepper
- 1/2 cup water
- Optional – 1 can of cream of mushroom soup (By adding this, it will change the recipe to not be gluten-free unless you purchase a gluten-free soup or make the recipe on the next page, page 39

DIRECTIONS:

1. Set up solar oven.
2. Rinse chicken and cut into bite sized pieces.
3. Add chicken to solar oven pan.
4. Stir together Mushrooms, water and seasonings (and optional can of soup).
5. Pour sauce over chicken.
6. Add pan with lid to solar oven and seal.
7. Let cook for 4-6 hours in oven or until it is no longer pink.

# Gluten-Free Cream of

# Mushroom Soup (Stove-top extra recipe)

- 16 ounces fresh sliced mushrooms
- 1/4 cup finely diced sweet onion
- 3 garlic cloves, minced or pressed
- 3 tablespoons butter
- 4 tablespoons sweet rice flour
- 1-1/2 cup water or chicken broth
- 1-1/2 cup milk
- 1/2 teaspoon salt
- 1/2 teaspoon pepper
- 2 Tablespoons butter

1. Sauté onions, mushrooms and garlic in butter until onions are transparent in a large pan on medium heat.
2. Sprinkle the rice flour over to form a roux.
3. Gradually stir in water/broth and then milk, stirring constantly until it thickens.
4. Season with salt and pepper.

# Jen's Easy Solar Oven

## Chicken Meal

### INGREDIENTS:

- 2-3 chicken breasts
- 1 cup uncooked quinoa, barley, or wild rice
- 3 cups V-8 juice or other vegetable juice
- 1/2 cup chopped onions
- 1 teaspoon salt
- 1 teaspoon Italian seasoning – page 186
- 1/2 teaspoon garlic powder
- 1/4 teaspoon chili powder – page 90
- 1/4 teaspoon pepper
- 1 cup cut veggies to your taste (carrots, zucchini, squash etc)

## DIRECTIONS:

1. Combine V-8 and quinoa, barley, or wild rice with the veggies, salt, and onions in your oven pots.
2. Add chicken breasts on top and sprinkle with seasonings.
3. Add pan with lid to solar oven and seal.
4. Cook 6-8 hours in full sun.

Quinoa is the perfect healthy replacement to pasta or rice in any dish. It has a mild flavor so you can spice it up to fit your own taste.

Tip: To create a creamy pasta substitute, add 1/2 of a small ripe mashed avocado and a dash of salt (to taste) to 2 cups of plain cooked quinoa. Mix well and serve.

# Cilantro Lime Chicken

## INGREDIENTS:

- 3-4 chicken breasts, chopped
- Juice from 3 limes
- 1 bunch fresh cilantro, chopped
- 4 Tomatillos, chopped (optional)
- 1 jalapeno, chopped (optional)
- 1 can of corn (undrained)
- 2 minced garlic cloves
- 1 red onion, chopped
- 1 cans of black beans, drained and rinsed

Serve with tortillas and your favorite toppings (sour cream, guacamole, salsa, and cheese. See page 58 for our guacamole recipe.

This recipe can be adjusted for a larger family too! Increase beans and corn to 2 cans each and use only 5-6 chicken breasts.

## DIRECTIONS:

1. Set up solar oven.
2. Rinse chicken, chop and add to solar oven pan.
3. Stir in all other ingredients.
4. Add pan with lid to solar oven and seal.
5. Let cook for 4-6 hours in oven or until chicken is no longer pink.

Every year we grow tomatillos in our garden. We always plant 4-6 plants.

In 2012, we had so many coming off of the vine, we ate them for every meal for 3 weeks straight. Our son Berlyn had so much fun picking them and peeling the husks.

# Honey Mustard Chicken

**INGREDIENTS:**

- 4 chicken breasts
- 1/4 cup mustard
- 1/4 cup honey – (We use local harvested honey from wild flowers that grow in our own back yard)
- 2 Tablespoons dried onion flakes
- 2 cloves of garlic, pressed
- 1-1/2 teaspoons curry powder

**DIRECTIONS:**

1. Set up solar oven.
2. Rinse chicken and cut into bite sized pieces.
3. Add chicken to solar oven pan.
4. Stir together mustard, honey, onions, garlic and curry powder.
5. Pour sauce over chicken.
6. Add pan with lid to solar oven and seal.
7. Let cook for 5-6 hours in oven or until the chicken is no longer pink.

# Cubed Chicken with Chiles

## INGREDIENTS:

- 4 chicken breasts, chopped
- 2 4-ounce cans of diced chilies or 4 large fresh chili peppers, diced
- 2 cloves fresh garlic pressed or 1 teaspoon garlic powder
- 1/2 cup water

This chicken is fantastic with tortillas, over rice and even alone.

Every year we grow heirloom chilies in our garden. This recipe tastes so good with fresh from the garden vegetables.

## DIRECTIONS:

1. Set up solar oven.
2. Rinse chicken, chop and add to solar oven pan.
3. Mix together water, chilies and garlic and pour over chicken.
4. Add pan with lid to solar oven and seal.
5. Let cook for 4-6 hours in oven or until chicken is no longer pink.

# Spinach Stuffed Chicken Breasts

## INGREDIENTS:

- 4 boneless, skinless chicken breasts
- 1/2 teaspoon salt
- 1 teaspoon pepper
- 3 cloves of garlic, pressed or minced
- 1-1/2 cups fresh spinach
- 1/3 cups fresh grated parmesan cheese
- 

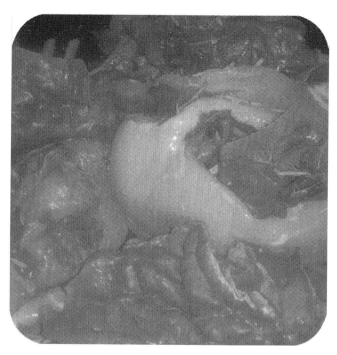

## DIRECTIONS:

1. Set up solar oven.
2. Rinse chicken and cut a slit in each piece to make a pocket in the chicken. Be careful not to cut completely through each piece.
3. Divide the spinach and cheese into 4 and stuff into the chicken pocket.
4. Add to solar oven pan, open side faced up.
5. Sprinkle with salt, pepper and garlic.
6. Add pan with lid to solar oven and seal.
7. Let cook for 4-6 hours in oven or until chicken is no longer pink.

# Roast with Sun-Dried Tomatoes

## INGREDIENTS:

- 3 pound chuck roast
- 6 carrots, quartered
- 8-10 fingerling potatoes
- 2 teaspoons coarsely ground salt
- 2 teaspoons freshly ground pepper
- 1 teaspoon garlic powder
- 1 cup water
- 1 Tablespoon olive oil
- 1/2 cup sun dried tomatoes

## DIRECTIONS:

1. Place the roast in the bottom of the solar oven pan and pour the water over the roast.
2. Sprinkle the roast with 1 t of ground pepper, the garlic powder and the dried tomatoes.
3. Add cut carrots, red onion and potatoes around the roast.
4. Sprinkle the remaining pepper and the olive oil over the vegetables.
5. Add pan with lid to solar oven and seal.
6. Let cook for 6-8 hours in oven or until cooked completely through.

# Pineapple Chicken

## INGREDIENTS:

- 4 chicken breasts
- 1 fresh pineapple or 2 cans of sliced pineapples
- 1/4 cup teriyaki sauce (Try using a Gluten-Free sauce to make this recipe Gluten-free)
- 1Tablespoon garlic powder
- Grated fresh ginger root or 1 teaspoon ground ginger
- 1teaspoon pepper

This dish is sure to become a family favorite.

In our house, the kids fight over who is getting another piece of pineapple especially when there is only a piece or two left. – Spears and pitchforks come out and most of the time, that means that dad gets the last piece of pineapple.

## DIRECTIONS:

1. Set up solar oven.
2. Rinse chicken and add to solar oven pan.
3. Mix teriyaki sauce, garlic powder, ginger and pepper and pour over chicken.
4. Arrange pineapple rings, slices, or chunks over top of chicken.
5. Add pan with lid to solar oven and seal.
6. Let cook for 4-6 hours in oven.

# Mediterranean Beef

## INGREDIENTS:

- 3 pounds beef roast, cut into small pieces
- 1 Tablespoon beef bouillon (if you are looking for a gluten-free recipe, make sure that your bouillon is GF)
- 1/2 teaspoon turmeric (I found this in the Hispanic seasonings section)
- 1/2 teaspoon black pepper
- 1/2 teaspoon ground cinnamon
- 1 teaspoon salt
- 1/2 teaspoon ground ginger or fresh grated ginger
- 1 can corn, drained
- 1 cup sweet peas (fresh) or 3/4 c frozen peas
- 1 Tablespoon garlic powder
- 2 cups water
- Optional: 1 cup pine nuts or almonds, toasted

## DIRECTIONS:

1. Combine all ingredients in a solar oven pan. Be sure to blend everything well as some of the seasonings are extremely strong.
2. Add pan with lid to solar oven and seal.
3. Let cook for 6-8 hours in oven or until cooked completely through.

My kids love this dish served over rice or quinoa (page 119) and served with a fresh green salad. If we have "left-overs" which doesn't happen often, we will serve this the next day in pita bread with yogurt sauce.

# Meatloaf

## INGREDIENTS:

- 2 pounds ground beef, chicken or turkey
- 2 large eggs, lightly beaten
- 3/4 cup bread crumbs (We use gluten free bread that I have air dried and ground up)
- 2 Tablespoons Worchester Sauce
- 1/4 cup grated carrots
- 1/4 cup grated zucchini
- 1 whole red onion chopped
- 1 teaspoon black pepper
- 1/2 teaspoon salt
- 1/2 cup chopped green onions
- 3 garlic cloves, pressed
- 1/2 cup minced cilantro
- 1/2 cup sun dried tomatoes, chopped

You can also fill the center of this meatloaf with cheese for a cheesy goodness. We will often add cheese and broccoli in the center to make a "surprise" meatloaf, a favorite of my 8 year old son Breckin.

## DIRECTIONS:

I never knew that I could make something so tasty in the solar oven. This was my very first dish ever created and attempted and it turned out great!!

1. Set up solar oven.
2. In a kitchen mixer, mix together all of ingredients until blended.
3. Form a loaf with the mixture and add to the solar oven pan.
4. Add pan with lid to solar oven and seal.
5. Let cook for 6-8 hours in oven or until cooked completely through.

**A story by Shelby Fullmer, our oldest daughter.**

One night, mom decided to make stuffed meatloaf with hidden vegetables. This time it was carrots, 2 cups of carrots to be exact. But instead of them being hidden, the carrots turned the loaf orange. I tried to act like I loved that meatloaf, but it was horrible. It was so horrible that even the dogs wouldn't eat it.

**Mom's recipe is ¼ cup of carrots for a reason.**

# Stuffed Bell Peppers

## INGREDIENTS:

- 6 large bell peppers
- 1 pound ground beef
- 1/3 cup long grain rice
- 1 onion, chopped
- 1 teaspoon ground pepper
- 1 clove of garlic, pressed
- 1/2 teaspoon salt
- one egg, beaten
- 2 tomatoes, chopped (including juice from cut tomatoes)
- 1/2 cup water

This dish is eaten often in our house especially in the summer time when bell peppers go on super sale at the grocery store and when our garden is in over abundance. Our two youngest kids often just eat the fillings out of the pepper. I am always hoping!

For topping:
- 1/2 cup grated Parmesan cheese (optional)
- 1/4 cup green onions, chopped

## DIRECTIONS:

1. Set up solar oven.
2. Cut the tops off of the bell peppers and pull out the seed bundle.
3. In a bowl mix remaining ingredients,
4. Divide the mixture and fill each bell pepper
5. Place filled peppers in solar oven pan.
6. Add pan with lid to solar oven and seal.
7. Let cook for 6-8 hours in oven or until cooked completely through.

# Apples & Pork

## INGREDIENTS:

- 4 apples, sliced
- 3 pounds of pork, cubed into 1 inch pieces
- 1 onion, sliced
- 1 cup brown sugar, packed
- 1-1/2 cups apple juice
- 1/2 cup apple cider vinegar
- 3 Tablespoon mustard
- 1 cup water

Breckin loves this dish so much that one day, he decided to help me out by cutting the apples. I gave him 4 apples and an apple slicer. The next thing I know, he sliced all 16 apples that I had sitting in the basket. We made baked apples for dessert that night too.

## DIRECTIONS:

1. Set up solar oven.
2. Add all ingredients to solar oven pan and stir.
3. Add pan with lid to solar oven and seal.
4. Let cook for 6-8 hours in oven or until pork is no longer pink.

# Jalapeno Cream Cheese Stuffed Chicken

## INGREDIENTS:

- 1- 4 ounce can diced jalapenos, chopped extra small
- 4 boneless skinless chicken breasts
- 1-8 ounce package cream cheese
- 1/2 teaspoon ground pepper
- 1/2 teaspoon dill
- 1/2 teaspoon thyme
- 1/2 teaspoon salt

## DIRECTIONS:

1. Set up solar oven.
2. With a meat tenderizer, flatten chicken breasts.
3. Mix together peppers, cream cheese, pepper, salt, dill and thyme.
4. Spread the cream cheese mixture on each of the chicken breasts.
5. Roll the chicken breasts.
6. Add pan with lid to solar oven and seal.
7. Let cook for 6-8 hours in oven or until cooked completely through.

# Beef Fajitas

**INGREDIENTS:**

- 2 pounds of flank steak sliced thin
- The juice of 2 limes
- 2 large bell peppers, sliced into thin strips
- 3 cloves of garlic, pressed
- 1 large red onion, sliced into thin strips.
- 1Tablespoon chili powder, page 90

**Guacamole**

(non-solar oven recipe)

Mix until blended

3 mashed avocados,

the juice of one lime,

¼ cup green onions,

1/4 cup cilantro,

2 Roma tomatoes, coarsely chopped,

1 clove of garlic, pressed or minced

1/4 cup of red onions, coarsely chopped,

1/2 teaspoon ground pepper

- 1/2 cup cilantro, coarsely chopped
- 1/2 cup sliced green onions

## DIRECTIONS:

1. Set up solar oven.
2. Add meat to solar oven pan.
3. Season meat with chili powder, garlic and lime juice.
4. Stir in green onions, cilantro, bell peppers and red onion slices to the pan.
5. Add pan with lid to solar oven and seal.
6. Let cook for 6-8 hours in oven or until cooked completely through.

Serve on tortillas with homemade guacamole, page 44 and sour cream. Many brands of corn Tortillas are gluten-free.

# Pulled Pork (or Chicken)

## INGREDIENTS:

- 1 4-5 pound pork butt roast or 4-6 boneless chicken breasts
- 1-1/2 teaspoons salt
- 1 teaspoon sugar
- 1-1/2 teaspoons coarsely ground black pepper
- 3 cloves of garlic, pressed or minced
- 1-1/2 teaspoon onion powder
- 1 can or bottle of beer

- 1 bottle of BBQ Sauce or recipe on page 60

### Homemade BBQ Sauce
(non-solar oven recipe)

- 1-6 ounce can tomato paste
- 1/2 cup apple cider vinegar
- 2 Tablespoon Worcestershire sauce – Check for GF versions
- 2 cloves of garlic, pressed or minced or 3/4 teaspoon garlic powder
- 1/3 cup honey (to taste)
- 1 teaspoon chili powder
- 1 teaspoon ground ginger
- 1/2 lime, juiced

Combine all ingredients on the stove in a saucepan for 7 minutes stirring

## DIRECTIONS:

1. Set up solar oven.
2. Add meat to solar oven pan.
3. Pour can of beer over the meat.
4. Season meat with salt, pepper. Sugar, garlic and onion powder.
5. Add pan with lid to solar oven and seal.
6. Let cook for 6-8 hours in oven or until cooked completely through.
7. Break apart meat with fork and add BBQ sauce and mix.

Serve on sandwich rolls.

# Wrapped Tilapia

### INGREDIENTS:

- 1 bundle of Swiss Chard, washed with stems removed
- The juice of one lemon
- 4-6 tilapia filets
- Pepper to taste

### DIRECTIONS:

1. Set up solar oven.
2. Pour lemon juice over the fish.
3. Sprinkle filets with pepper.
4. Wrap a piece of Swiss chard around each fish and place each wrapped filet in the solar oven pan.
5. Add pan with lid to solar oven and seal.
6. Let cook for 4-6 hours.

### Mahi Mahi with Pineapple Salsa

Add 2 mahi mahi fillets into your solar oven pan. Sprinkle with Caribbean jerk seasonings. Add to solar oven pan, seal in oven and bake for 4 hours or until fish is finished.

For Pineapple Salsa: Core and/or chop 1 pineapple, 4 green onions, 3 tomatillos, 2 roma tomatoes, 1 red onion and 1/2 cup cilantro and combine in a bowl. Serve salsa over fish.

# Dill Lemon White Fish

## INGREDIENTS:

- 4 (5-oz.) fresh tilapia fillets
- 1 teaspoon salt
- 1/2 teaspoon pepper
- 1 lemon, sliced
- 2 tablespoons fresh dill
- 2 tablespoons fresh parsley
- 2 tablespoons butter

## DIRECTIONS:

1. Set up solar oven.
2. Add fillets to solar oven pans.
3. Sprinkle fillets with pepper, dill, and parsley.
4. Top fillets with butter and place lemon slices on top of the fillets
5. Add pan with lid to solar oven and seal.
6. Let cook for 4-6 hours.

# Bleu Cheese Steak Roll-up

## INGREDIENTS:

- 1-1/2 pounds of round tip steak, thinly cut
- 1/2 cup red wine
- 1/2 cup soy sauce
- 2 Tablespoons Worcestershire sauce
- 4 cloves garlic, pressed or minced
- 16 ounces of blue cheese

## DIRECTIONS:

1. Set up solar oven.
2. Mix together red wine, soy sauce, Worcestershire sauce and garlic.
3. Lay out beef on a cutting board.
4. Sprinkle 3-4 ounces of bleu cheese on the meat and roll each piece of meat.
5. Add meat to solar oven pan.
6. Finish all meat and add all pieces to the solar oven pan.
7. Pour sauce over the meat.
8. Add pan with lid to solar oven and seal.
9. Let cook for 6+ hours or until meat is done.

# Chicken Cordon Bleu Roll-up

## INGREDIENTS:

- 4 boneless skinless chicken breasts, washed trimmed and pounded flat
- 8 slices of Swiss cheese
- 8 slices of deli cut ham
- Tooth picks

## DIRECTIONS:

1. Set up solar oven.
2. On a separate plate, lay chicken breast out flat.
3. Layer ham and cheese on top of chicken breast.
4. Roll chicken and securing with toothpick and add to solar oven pan.
5. Repeat with each chicken breast.
6. Add pan with lid to solar oven and seal.
7. Let cook for 6+ hours or until meat is done.

# Hobo Stew

The following recipe is for ONE hobo stew which is ONE serving. We make 10+ when we go camping and these can be thrown in your solar oven after lunch for dinner or even on a campfire or grill. Note: No hobos were harmed in making this, says Poppie.

## INGREDIENTS:

- 1 hamburger patty
- 1/3 cup hash browns or home style potatoes, thawed
- 1/3 cup frozen mixed veggies, thawed
- 1 teaspoon teriyaki or 1 tablespoon of BBQ sauce – page 60
- Salt and pepper to taste
- Aluminum foil

## DIRECTIONS:

1. Set up solar oven.
2. Lay out square of aluminum foil and place hamburger patty in middle of foil.
3. Sprinkle with salt and pepper.
4. Place potatoes and vegetables on top of patty.
5. Sprinkle again with salt and pepper.
6. Add sauce to top of "mound."

7. Pull up corners of aluminum foil to form a "bundle" and twist foil to seal.

8. Add bundle to solar oven and seal oven.

9. Let cook for 4 hours in oven or until meat is cooked.

*Kids enjoying Hobo Stew while camping*

# Kielbasa Vegetable Bake

## INGREDIENTS:

- 1- 14 ounce package turkey kielbasa, cut into 1/4 inch rounds (Check for Gluten Free at the store)
- 1 green bell pepper, diced
- 1 yellow, red or orange bell pepper, diced
- 1 red onion, diced
- 3 small or 2 large potatoes, peeled and diced
- olive oil
- salt and pepper

## DIRECTIONS:

1. Set up solar oven.
2. Stir in all ingredients in the solar oven pan.
3. Add pan to solar oven and seal.
4. Let cook for 4-6 hours in oven.

# Brown Sugar Ham

## INGREDIENTS:

- 2 cup brown sugar, divided
- 7 to 8 pound spiral ham
- 20-oumce can pineapple tidbits or 2 cups fresh pineapple, cubed

## DIRECTIONS:

1. Set up solar oven.
2. Pre slice ham and layer in solar oven pans
3. If using more than one pan, divide brown sugar and pineapple in half.
4. Sprinkle brown sugar over ham.
5. Pour pineapple chunks over ham.
6. Add pans to solar oven and seal.
7. Let cook for 6-8 hours in oven.

# Tips and Tricks for Meat in your Solar Oven

You can cook any type of meat in your solar oven.

My sister, Jen, normally just cooks her meat and doesn't follow recipes. She says that a solar oven "makes a mean whole chicken."

Some of the "plain meats" that you can cook include:

• Chicken Breasts or other parts including legs and thighs, bone in or boneless
  • Beef roasts
  • Fish fillets, non-breaded
  • Pork chops or roasts
  • Any game meat, including elk, deer and antelope
  • Sausages and kielbasas

You do not need to add water to your meat. Do not overcook however or it can become dry.

Season your meat the way that you want! Try new herbs or combinations! We found some really tasty Caribbean Jerk seasoning that tastes AMAZING on Chicken!

# Add your Own Meat Dish

Title: _____

## INGREDIENTS:

_____          _____
_____          _____
_____          _____
_____          _____
_____          _____
_____          _____
_____          _____

## DIRECTIONS:

_____
_____
_____
_____
_____
_____
_____
_____
_____
_____
_____
_____
_____

# Add your Own Meat Dish

Title: _____

INGREDIENTS:

_____    _____

_____    _____

_____    _____

_____    _____

_____    _____

_____    _____

DIRECTIONS:

_____

_____

_____

_____

_____

_____

_____

_____

_____

_____

_____

_____

_____

# Add your Own Meat Dish

Title: _____

## INGREDIENTS:

_____  _____
_____  _____
_____  _____
_____  _____
_____  _____
_____  _____
_____  _____

## DIRECTIONS:

_____
_____
_____
_____
_____
_____
_____
_____
_____
_____
_____
_____
_____

# Add your Own Meat Dish

Title: _____

INGREDIENTS:

_____     _____
_____     _____
_____     _____
_____     _____
_____     _____
_____     _____
_____     _____

DIRECTIONS:

_____
_____
_____
_____
_____
_____
_____
_____
_____
_____
_____
_____
_____
_____
_____

# Add your Own Meat Dish

Title: _____

## INGREDIENTS:

_____          _____

_____          _____

_____          _____

_____          _____

_____          _____

_____          _____

_____          _____

## DIRECTIONS:

_____

_____

_____

_____

_____

_____

_____

_____

_____

_____

_____

_____

_____

We love that our solar oven is so easy to set up. Both Griffen and Elwyn, our 12 and 10 year olds, can set it up and get food cooking with ease.

We can often find one of the kids in the kitchen creating something to the solar oven. Here is Shelby making granola as a snack. Granola – page 15, only take 1 hour to bake and about 15 minutes to cool.

# CASSEROLES

I am always being asked "Are all of those kids yours?" Often times, I will answer, "Where did that one come from?" I have some CRAZY answers for them on those questions.

I am also often asked how I cook for all of these kids... Casseroles, definitely casseroles are the way to go!

- Chicken and Rice
- Parmesan Chicken Bake
  - Homemade Marinara Sauce
- Green Bean Casserole
- Shelby's Tator Tot Casserole
- Sloppy Joe Casserole
- Pizza Casserole
- Enchiladas
  - Homemade Enchilada Sauce
- Spinach Casserole
- Hamburger & Potato Casserole
- Black Bean Tortilla Bake
- Chili Rellano Casserole
- Loaded Baked Potato Casserole

# Chicken and Rice Casserole

## INGREDIENTS:

- 1-1/2 cups rice (not instant)
- 3 cups water
- 2 chicken breasts, uncooked, washed, and cubed into small, bite-sized pieces
- 1 cup frozen mixed vegetables
- 1 can of cream of mushroom soup – or homemade for a gluten-free version, recipe on page 39
- 1 cup cheddar cheese grated
- 1 teaspoon salt
- 1 teaspoon pepper
- 1 teaspoon paprika

This is a family favorite that we make in our kitchen oven in the winter time when there is no sun out and in the solar oven in the summer.

This is one of the family favorites that we had to first convert to a gluten-free. Now that we have, this is one of Trystan's favorite dishes.

## DIRECTIONS:

1. Add rice and water in the bottom of the solar oven pan.
2. Add chicken, mixed vegetables, cream of mushroom soup, and seasonings.
3. Top with cheese.
4. Add pan with lid to solar oven and seal.
5. Let cook for 6-8 hours in oven or until cooked completely through.

# Parmesan Chicken Bake

## INGREDIENTS:

- 4 boneless, skinless chicken breasts, washed and cubed
- 1 jar of Marinara sauce or 4 cups of homemade sauce
- 1 cup grated mozzarella cheese
- 1/2 cup grated parmesan cheese
- 1 cup panko, bread crumbs or gluten free bread crumbs
- 2 tablespoons of butter or coconut oil, melted
- 3 Tablespoons fresh parsley
- 2 Tablespoons fresh oregano
- 2 cloves garlic, pressed or minced

## DIRECTIONS:

1. Set up solar oven.
2. Place cubes chicken in solar oven pan.
3. Pour the marinara sauce over the chicken.
4. Sprinkle the mozzarella cheese over the sauce.
5. In a separate bowl, mix together the bread crumbs, butter, and herbs until well blended.
6. Stir in the parmesan cheese to the bread mixture and then sprinkle the mixture over the top of the chicken.
7. Add pan with lid to solar oven and seal.
8. Let cook for 4-6 hours in oven or until chicken is no longer pink.

Serve over noodles or plain with cheese toast or sour dough bread.

## Homemade Marinara Sauce

### (Stove-top extra recipe)

This recipe was given to me by my grandmother. LOVED eating pasta with this sauce at her house as a child!!

- 1/2 cup of olive oil
- 1 medium onion chopped
- 2 cloves of garlic minced
- 1/4 cup fresh basil, chopped
- 2 Tablespoon fresh parsley, chopped
- 1 teaspoon dried oregano
- 2- 28oz cans of crushed tomatoes
- 1 teaspoon salt
- 1/2 teaspoon black pepper
- 1 -2 Tablespoon balsamic vinegar

### Directions

1. In a saucepan, heat the oil on medium heat. Add the onion and garlic and sauté until onions are translucent.
2. Add the fresh basil, fresh parsley and dried oregano and stir continuously for 1 minute.
3. Add the two cans of crushed tomatoes, salt and pepper and stir everything so it's nicely mixed and bring the sauce to a boil.
4. Simmer for 25 minutes and then add vinegar. Let boil for 5 more minutes.

# Green Bean Casserole

## INGREDIENTS:

- 1 16-ounce bag of frozen green beans, thawed
- 1 8-ounce package of fresh mushrooms, sliced
- 1 small onion, diced
- 1-1/2 Tablespoons parsley
- 1 can of cream of mushroom soup or a home-made sauce on page 39
- 1 cup shredded cheddar cheese
- 1/2 cup almonds, sliced
- 1 teaspoon black pepper
- 2 Tablespoons teriyaki sauce
- 1-2.8 ounce can canned French fried onions

## DIRECTIONS:

1. Set up solar oven.
2. Add all ingredients, except the French fried onion into the solar oven pan and mix thoroughly.
3. Sprinkle fried onions on top.
4. Add pan with lid to solar oven and seal.
5. Let cook for 4-6 hours in oven or until cooked completely through.

# Shelby's Tater Tot Casserole

## INGREDIENTS:

- 1 pound ground beef
- 4 cups tater tots
- 2 cups mixes vegetables
- 1 can of cream of mushroom soup or a home-made sauce - page 39
- 2 teaspoons of Italian seasoning – page 186
- 1 teaspoon salt
- 1 teaspoon pepper
- 1 cup cheddar cheese, grated,

## DIRECTIONS:

1. Set up solar oven.
2. Press raw hamburger into bottom of pan.
3. Spread cream of mushroom soup on top of meat.
4. Next, layer vegetables on top of soup.
5. Layer Tater Tots evenly on top of the soup.
6. Sprinkle cheese on top of tater tots.
7. Lastly, sprinkle all seasonings on the top of everything.
8. Add pan with lid to solar oven and seal.
9. Let cook for 4-6 hours.

# Sloppy Joe Casserole

INGREDIENTS:
- 1 32-ounce bag of hash browns
- 1 egg, beaten
- 1 pound ground beef
- 1 onion, chopped
- 2 cups cheddar cheese, grated and divided equally
- 1 can sloppy joe sauce
- 1 teaspoon salt
- 1 teaspoon black pepper

DIRECTIONS:

1. Set up solar oven.
2. Stir together hash browns, egg, salt, pepper, and 1 cup of cheese and layer in the bottom of the solar oven pan.
3. Crumble hamburger meat and onion over the potatoes.
4. Pour over the sloppy joe sauce and sprinkle on the remaining cheese.
5. Add pan with lid to solar oven and seal.
6. Let cook for 4-6 hours in oven or until cooked completely through.

# Pizza Casserole

## INGREDIENTS:

- 1 Box (16 oz) Spiral Pasta, uncooked
- 1 pound lean ground beef (Can also use ground turkey or chicken as well)
- 1 onion, chopped
- 1 clove garlic, pressed or minced
- 1 green bell pepper, chopped
- 1-1/2 cups sliced pepperoni
- 32 ounces pasta sauce
- 1 cup water
- 1 cup shredded mozzarella cheese

## DIRECTIONS:

1. Layer all ingredients in above order to a solar oven pots.
2. Add pan to solar oven and seal.
3. Let cook all day in oven.

Serve with Salad and Bread Sticks

Making a gluten-free alternative can be very easy.

Replace the pasta with a high quality gluten free pasta and pepperoni. Be sure to check the ingredients in your pasta sauce as well if you are not making your own.

# Enchiladas

## INGREDIENTS:

- 1 pound ground beef
- 1-8 ounce block of cream cheese, cubed
- 1/2 cup chopped green pepper.
- 1 - 14 ounce can Enchilada sauce, red or green (check that your enchilada sauce is GF – We make our own red sauce – see recipe on page 87)
- 1/2 teaspoon black pepper
- 1-1/2 teaspoon chili powder – page 90
- 1/2 cup green onions
- 1/2 cup cilantro chopped
- 1 can of tomatoes, diced
- 2 cups shredded Mexican blend cheese
- 16 corn tortillas

## DIRECTIONS:

1. Set up solar oven
2. Layer tortillas on the bottom of the solar oven pan.
3. Top tortillas with 1/2 of the hamburger meat and 1/2 of the cream cheese.
4. Sprinkle with half of the seasonings.
5. Add 1/2 of the can of tomatoes, ¼ cup of green onions, 1/4 cup of cilantro.
6. Repeat steps 2-5 in the pan.
7. Add can of sauce on the top of the food in the pan.

8. Top with cheese

9. Add pan with lid to solar oven and seal and let cook for 6-8 hours.

### Homemade Red Enchilada Sauce

(stove-top extra recipe)

- 2 Tablespoons Butter
- 1/2 cup onions
- 1 clove garlic, pressed
- 1-16 ounce can tomatoes, diced & undrained
- 1-8 ounce can of tomato sauce
- 1-1/2 teaspoon sugar
- 1 teaspoon cumin
- 1-4 ounce can of green chilies
- 1/2 teaspoon oregano
- 1/2 teaspoon basil
- 3/4 teaspoon salt
- 1/2 teaspoon chili powder

Melt butter in saucepan on stove. Add onions and garlic and sauté until tender. Add tomatoes, tomato sauce, chilies, sugar and seasonings. Simmer for about 15 minutes until heated.

# Spinach Casserole

## INGREDIENTS:

- 2-16 ounce packages of frozen spinach, thawed, chopped and dried
- 1 cup onions, minced
- 1 cup cottage cheese
- 16 ounces of cream cheese, cubed
- 2 cups mozzarella cheese, grated
- 2 eggs, beaten well
- 1/4 cup flour
- 1 stick of butter
- 1 clove garlic, pressed or minced or 3/4 teaspoon garlic powder
- 1 teaspoon pepper
- 1/2 teaspoon salt

> To make this into a gluten-free recipe, change the flour to coconut flour and add 2 additional eggs to the recipe.

## DIRECTIONS:

1. Set up solar oven.
2. Stir all ingredients together, blend well.
3. Add pan with lid to solar oven and seal.
4. Let cook for 4-6 hours.
5. Stir well before serving.

# Hamburger & Potato Casserole

## INGREDIENTS:

- 1 pound ground hamburger
- 4-6 potatoes, sliced thin.
- 1/2 cup mushrooms, sliced
- 1 red onion, minced
- 1 teaspoon pepper
- 1 teaspoon salt
- 1 can of cream of mushroom soup – homemade recipe - page 39
- 1/2 cup milk
- 1 teaspoon parsley
- 1 cup cheddar cheese, shredded

## DIRECTIONS:

1. Set up solar oven.
2. In bowl, combine cream of mushroom soup, onion, milk, salt and pepper.
3. Layer potatoes, mushrooms, hamburger meat and soup mix in the solar oven pan.
4. Add pan with lid to solar oven and seal.
5. Let cook for 4-6 hours.

# Black Bean Tortilla Bake

## INGREDIENTS:

- 1 pound ground beef
- 1/2 cup onion, chopped
- 1-15 ounce can of black beans, drained
- 1-16 ounce can of tomatoes, diced
- 1 can of corn, drained (optional)
- 3/4 cup enchilada sauce – page 87
- 1-1/2 teaspoon of chili powder – page 90
- 1 teaspoon cumin
- 1 teaspoon black pepper
- 1-4 ounce can of green chilies or 2 fresh chilies, finely diced
- 8 ounce block of cream cheese, cubed
- 6 flour tortillas

**Chili Powder**

Making your own chili powder is very easy. We grow our own chilies in our garden. When we have an over-abundance, we dehydrate and then grind them after they are dried. I have found that the best grinder for herbs is a coffee grinder. I found mine for $1 at a yard sale too!!

# DIRECTIONS:

1. Set up solar oven.
2. Spread cream cheese on 3 of the tortillas.
3. Divide the green chilies between the 3 and spread on the cream cheese.
4. Top with other tortillas to make 3 "sandwiches" and set aside.
5. Mix together the seasonings (chili powder, cumin, and pepper) into the enchilada sauce, beans, corn, onions and tomatoes in a separate bowl.
6. Line the solar oven pan with one of the tortillas.
7. Layer 1/3 of the meat on top of the tortilla along with 1/3 of the sauce mixture.
8. Layer the next tortilla sandwich onto the mixture in the solar oven pan and repeat the next layer of meat and sauce.
9. Layer the 3rd tortilla and the last 1/3 of the meat and sauce.
10. Add pan with lid to solar oven and seal.
11. Let cook for 4-6 hours.

Slice and serve with guacamole (page 44) or sour cream.

# Chili Rellano Casserole

- 9 fire roasted chilies, stems cut off, peeled and seeded (You might want to wear gloves while preparing your chilies – we speak from experience!)
- 3 cups shredded cheddar cheese or colby jack
- 8 ounces of cream cheese, cubed
- 1 large onion, diced
- 6 eggs
- 1 can evaporated milk
- 1/4 cup flour
- 1 tsp baking powder
- 1 teaspoon salt
- 2 teaspoons black pepper
- 1 teaspoon chili powder – page 90

## DIRECTIONS:

1. Set up solar oven
2. Line solar oven pan with 3 of the chilies.
3. Add cream cheese to solar oven pan and cover with 3 more chilies.
4. Next, layer 1 cup of the cheese and onions and add the last 3 chilies on top of the cheese.
5. In a separate bowl, mix together 1 cup of cheese, 6 eggs, evaporated milk, flour, baking powder, salt, black pepper and chili powder.
6. Top with remaining cheese.
7. Add pan with lid to solar oven and seal.
8. Let cook for 4-6 hours or until eggs are cooked through.

# Loaded Potato Casserole

## INGREDIENTS:

- 6 russet potatoes, scrubbed and sliced into 1/4-inch thick rounds
- 2 garlic cloves, pressed or minced
- 1 cup shredded cheddar cheese
- 1 cup shredded monterey jack cheese
- 8 slices bacon, cooked to desired crispiness and crumbled
- 2 cups milk
- 2 large eggs
- 4 green onions, sliced
- 1 teaspoon salt,
- 1 teaspoon pepper
- 2 tablespoons chopped fresh parsley

## DIRECTIONS:

1. Set up solar oven
2. Layer half the potatoes in the solar oven pan.
3. Sprinkle shredded cheeses, bacon and green onions,
4. Layer the rest of the potato slices on top, overlapping slightly
5. In a separate mixing bowl, whisk together milk, eggs, salt and pepper.
6. Pour the milk mixture over potatoes.
7. Sprinkle Parsley over the top
8. Top with remaining cheese.
9. Add pan with lid to solar oven and seal.
    1. Let cook for 6-8 hours or until potatoes are cooked

Serve with a dollop of sour cream.

# Add your Own Casserole Dish

Title: _____

INGREDIENTS:

_____    _____
_____    _____
_____    _____
_____    _____
_____    _____
_____    _____

DIRECTIONS:

_____
_____
_____
_____
_____
_____
_____
_____
_____
_____
_____
_____
_____

# Add your Own Casserole Dish

Title: _____

## INGREDIENTS:

_____        _____

_____        _____

_____        _____

_____        _____

_____        _____

_____        _____

_____        _____

## DIRECTIONS:

_____

_____

_____

_____

_____

_____

_____

_____

_____

_____

_____

_____

_____

# Add your Own Casserole Dish

Title: _____

## INGREDIENTS:

_____     _____
_____     _____
_____     _____
_____     _____
_____     _____
_____     _____

## DIRECTIONS:

_____
_____
_____
_____
_____
_____
_____
_____
_____
_____
_____
_____

# Add your Own Casserole Dish

Title: _____

## INGREDIENTS:

_____        _____
_____        _____
_____        _____
_____        _____
_____        _____
_____        _____
_____        _____

## DIRECTIONS:

_____
_____
_____
_____
_____
_____
_____
_____
_____
_____
_____
_____

I remember coming home one day and my dogs were missing, I went around back and found my 3 black labs, chowing down on my stuffed spinach chicken. They loved it and it smelled so good. I sat down and cried. That's what I wanted for dinner!

The next week, I attempted to make the same dish and found that all three of my dogs were hovering again on that dish and managed to open my solar oven for a second time. "NOOOOO!!!"

I have had my dogs for many years and they have been around our solar ovens from day 1. We have never had them open the ovens or help themselves before, nor have they done it with any other dish but the spinach stuffed chicken.

All I can say, is they have GREAT taste. I now will never make that dish if I know that I am leaving the house!

# SIDES

- Baked Potatoes or Baked Sweet Potatoes
- Cheesy Potatoes
- Stuffing
- Baked Brussels Sprouts
- Baked Beans
- Rice
- Chicken Flavored Rice
- Parmesan Cheese Herb Rice
- Baked Butternut Squash
- Ranch Beans
- Rosemary Potatoes
- Mashed Cauliflower
- Honey Carrots
- Buttered Turnips
- "Canned" Veggies
- Sweet Potatoes with Walnuts
- Quinoa
  - Quinoa Salad
- Mac'n'Cheese Bake
  - Traditional Mac'n'Cheese
- Roasted Garlic
- Baked Radish and Turnips
- Garlic Endives

# Baked Potatoes

# Or Baked Sweet Potatoes

## INGREDIENTS:

- 4 large potatoes – baking potatoes or sweet potatoes, scrubbed
- 1Tablespoon olive oil (total for potatoes, not each)
- Aluminum foil

## DIRECTIONS:

1. Set up solar oven.
2. Lay out square of aluminum foil.
3. Place potato in the middle and drizzle with olive oil.
4. Wrap the foil around the potato and seal.
5. Add to pan.
6. Add pan with lid to solar oven and seal.
7. Let cook for 6-8 hours or until potatoes are soft.

Serve with your favorite potato toppings.

# Cheesy Potato Bake

## INGREDIENTS:

- 6-8 large potatoes, washed and thinly sliced
- 1-1/2 cups grated cheddar cheese
- 1/2 cup milk
- 1/4 cup green onions chopped fine
- 4 Tablespoons butter, divided
- 1 teaspoon salt
- 1/2 teaspoon smoked paprika or chili powder (page 90)

## DIRECTIONS:

1. Set up solar oven.
2. Stir in all ingredients in the solar oven pan.
3. Add pan to solar oven and seal.
4. Let cook for 4-6 hours in oven.

# Stuffing

## INGREDIENTS:

- 16 cups 1-inch bread cubes, (white, wheat, sour dough or even gluten free bread. )
- 1-1/4 cup chicken stock
- 2 cups medium-diced yellow onion
- 2 cups medium-diced celery
- 3 granny smith apples, unpeeled, cored and large diced
- 3/4 cup cranberries
- 1/2 cup sliced almonds
- 2 tablespoons chopped flat-leaf parsley
- 1-1/2 teaspoons minced fresh rosemary leaves
- 2 teaspoons salt
- 1 teaspoon freshly ground black pepper

## DIRECTIONS:

1. Set up solar oven.
2. Stir together all ingredients except the chicken stock in the solar oven pan.
3. Gently pour the chicken stock over the mixture.
4. Add pan to solar oven and seal.
5. Let cook for 4-6 hours in oven.

# Baked Brussels Sprouts

## INGREDIENTS:

- 1 pound Brussels sprouts
- 4 Tablespoons butter, melted
- 1 Tablespoon Dijon mustard
- 1 Tablespoon Worchester Sauce
- 1/2 teaspoon kosher salt
- 1/24 teaspoon black pepper
- 1/4 cup water

I used to get the "EEEWWWW" response from the kids when I said that I was going to make Brussels sprouts for dinner until we started making this version.

## DIRECTIONS:

1. Set up solar oven.
2. Blend together melted butter, mustard, Worchester sauce, salt, pepper. Set aside.
3. Wash Brussels sprouts, and cut in half.
4. Place sprouts in pan and pour sauce over.
5. Add pan to solar oven and seal.
6. Let cook for 2-4 hours in oven.
7. Stir before serving.

# Baked Beans

## INGREDIENTS:

- 1 lb navy beans, dried
- 8 slices thick-cut bacon, cooked and cut into pieces
- 1 sweet onion, medium, chopped
- 1 clove garlic, pressed or minced
- 2 cups water
- 3/4 cup barbecue sauce or the recipe from page 60
- 3/4  cup brown sugar, packed
- 1/4 cup ketchup
- 2 Tablespoons molasses
- 1/2 cup bourbon
- 1-1/2 Tablespoons ground mustard
- 1/4 cup apple cider vinegar

## DIRECTIONS:

**Soak beans overnight in water.**

1. Set up solar oven.
2. Drain and rinse beans.
3. Add all ingredients into your solar oven pan and stir.
4. Add pan with lid to solar oven and seal.
5. Let cook for 8+ hours until beans are soft and cooked.

# Rice

## INGREDIENTS:

- 1 cup rice plus 2 cups of water (We make 3 cups of rice at a time plus 6 cups of water to feed our entire crew.)

The rice will soak up the water as it is cooking. Do NOT use instant rice, but rather use long grain, white or wild or brown rice. We have tried the Black rice in ours as well and it works great.

## DIRECTIONS:

1. Set up solar oven.
2. Place rice and water in the solar oven pan.
3. Add pan with lid to solar oven and seal.
4. Let cook for 3-4 hours.

# Chicken Flavored Rice

## INGREDIENTS:

- 1 cup rice
- 2 cups of chicken broth
- 1 teaspoon lemon zest
- 1 teaspoon black pepper

Do NOT use instant rice, but rather use long grain, white, wild or brown.

## DIRECTIONS:

1. Set up solar oven.
2. Place rice and chicken broth in the solar oven pan.
3. Sprinkle with the zest and pepper.
4. Add pan with lid to solar oven and seal.
5. Let cook for 3-4 hours.

# Parmesan Cheese Herb Rice

## INGREDIENTS:

- 1 cup rice
- 2 cups water
- 1 cup milk
- 1 cup parmesan cheese
- 1 Tablespoon  Italian seasoning – page 186

Do NOT use instant rice, but rather use long grain, white or wild. We have tried the Black rice in ours as well and it works great.

## DIRECTIONS:

1. Set up solar oven.
2. Place rice and water, milk, cheese and seasonings in the solar oven pan.
3. Add pan with lid to solar oven and seal.
4. Let cook for 3-4 hours.
5. Stir well before serving.

# Baked Butternut Squash

## INGREDIENTS:

- 1 large butternut squash, peeled and cubed
- 4 Tablespoon butter in 1 Tablespoon pats
- 1 sprig of rosemary, leaves removed from stem
- 1 teaspoon coarse salt

## DIRECTIONS:

1. Set up solar oven.
2. Place squash in the solar oven pan.
3. Place the 4 pats of butter on top of the squash along with the rosemary leaves and salt.
4. Add pan with lid to solar oven and seal.
5. Let cook for 4-6 hours.

# Ranch Beans

## INGREDIENTS:

- 1 pound of dried pinto beans
- 4 chilies, stems and seeds removed
- 4 cloves of garlic, pressed
- 1 onion, diced
- 1-15 oz. can of tomatoes
- 1/4 cup brown sugar
- 2 teaspoons apple cider vinegar
- 1 teaspoon paprika
- 1 teaspoon cumin
- 1 teaspoon oregano
- 2 cups of water
- 5 cups of beef broth
- Salt and black pepper to taste

## DIRECTIONS:

**Soak beans overnight in water.**

1. Set up solar oven.
2. Drain and rinse beans.
3. Add all ingredients into your solar oven pan and stir.
4. Add pan with lid to solar oven and seal.
5. Let cook for 8+ hours until beans are soft and cooked.

 # Shelby's Rosemary Potatoes

## INGREDIENTS:

- 6-8 potatoes, washed and sliced long ways in half
- 1 teaspoon coarse salt
- 4 Tablespoons butter, divided
- 2 sprigs of fresh rosemary, leaves removed from stem

We grow all of our own fresh herbs at our home in pots on the patio. We simply walk outside and clip what we need for the meal. Many of our plants come back every year including our chives and cilantro. We move our plants into our greenhouse in the wintertime and water only once a week.

## DIRECTIONS:

1. Set up solar oven.
2. Lay potatoes in pan skin side down.
3. Add sliced butter to top of potatoes.
4. Sprinkle with rosemary and salt.
5. Add pan with lid to solar oven and seal.
6. Let cook for 4-6 hours.

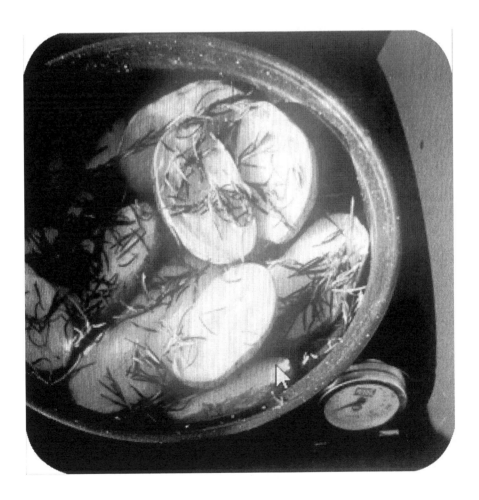

# Mashed Cauliflower

INGREDIENTS FOR THE SOLAR OVEN:
- 1 head of cauliflower, chopped into small florets
- 1 cup water

DIRECTIONS:

1. Set up solar oven.
2. Add cauliflower and water into solar oven pan
3. Add pan with lid to solar oven and seal.
4. Let cook for 4-6 hours.

Once cooked through, add
- 1 clove of garlic, pressed,
- 1/4 cup Greek yogurt
- 1/2 teaspoon salt,
- 1/ 2 teaspoon ground pepper,
- 1/4 cup milk,
- 2 tablespoon butter

Mash everything together to make a cream with the consistency of "mashed potatoes." Top with cheese if desired.

# Honey Carrots

## INGREDIENTS:

- 1 pound carrots, sliced
- 1 teaspoon salt
- 1/4 cup honey
- 1/4 cup water
- 2 Tablespoons brown sugar
- 2 Tablespoons of butter divided into 6 pieces

## DIRECTIONS:

1. Place carrots in the solar oven pan.
2. Stir together the salt, honey, water and brown sugar.
3. Add pats of butter on top of carrots.
4. Pour mixture on top of carrots and butter
5. Add pan with lid to solar oven and seal.
6. Let cook for 4-6 hours.

# Buttered Turnips

- 4 purple topped turnips, washed and grated
- 4 Tablespoon butter, softened
- 2 cloves garlic, pressed or minced
- 1 teaspoon pepper
- 1/2 teaspoon salt
- 4 green onion, finely chopped

DIRECTIONS:

1. Place grated turnips, butter, garlic, salt and pepper in the solar oven pan.
2. Mix well.
3. Add pan with lid to solar oven and seal.
4. Let cook for 4-6 hours.

# Canned

# Vegetables

I love that I can utilize my solar oven to heat up simple items like canned or frozen veggies. Two cans of corn will take about 2 hours to heat in the solar oven. We will often times add our side dish to our oven in the morning at the same time as our main dish. Frozen veggies work well too, but will take additional time to heat up.

## INGREDIENTS:

- 1 Can of Corn, peas or mixed vegetables, drained, or 10-12 ounce package of frozen vegetables
- 1/2 cup water
- Optional butter
- Optional salt and pepper to taste

## DIRECTIONS:

1. Empty can of vegetables, drained, into the solar oven pan.
2. Add any ingredients as you would on your stove top, such as butter, salt, pepper, other seasonings.
3. Add pan with lid to solar oven and seal.
4. Let cook for 2+ hours.

# Sweet Potatoes
# with Walnuts

## INGREDIENTS:

- 4 sweet potatoes, peeled and sliced into bit sized chunks
- 1/2 cup walnuts, crushed
- 4 Tablespoons butter
- Optional salt and pepper

## DIRECTIONS:

1. Set up solar oven.
2. Lay sweet potatoes out in solar oven pan.
3. Add sliced butter to top of potatoes.
4. Sprinkle walnuts on top of the potatoes.
5. Add pan with lid to solar oven and seal.
6. Let cook for 4-6 hours.

# Quinoa

## INGREDIENTS:

- 1 cup quinoa plus 2 cups of water (We make 3 cups of quinoa at a time plus 6 cups of water to feed our entire crew.)

## DIRECTIONS:

1. Set up solar oven.
2. Rinse quinoa (Trust me, it tastes much better!).
3. Place quinoa and water in the solar oven pan.
4. Add pan with lid to solar oven and seal.
5. Let cook for 2-3 hours or until all of the water is soaked up.

To make this is cheesy dish, stir in 1/2 cup of cheese after it is cooked and stir until melted.

# Southwest Quinoa Salad

## INGREDIENTS:

- 2 cup cooked quinoa (Use recipe on page 119 to cook the quinoa)
- 2 small avocados, ripe but not mushy, peeled and cubed
- 1 red bell pepper, chopped
- 1 small red onion, finely chopped
- 1 can of black beans or 1-1/2 cup of cooked black beans (you can cook these in your solar oven too!)
- 2 teaspoons curry powder
- 1/4 cup chopped fresh cilantro
- 1 lime, juiced
- 1/4 cup toasted sliced almonds
- 1/2 cup grated carrots
- 1/2 cup dried cranberries or raisins
- salt and ground black pepper to taste

## SALAD DRESSING:

- 1/4 cup fresh lime juice
- 1/4 cup red wine vinegar
- 1/4 cup olive oil
- 2 cloves of garlic, pressed or minced garlic
- 1 tablespoon honey
- 1/2 teaspoon kosher salt
- 1/4 teaspoon freshly cracked black pepper

-

## DIRECTIONS:

1. Using cooked Quinoa (Using recipe from page 119).
2. In a large bowl, stir together all salad ingredients together.
3. In a separate bowl, mix together salad dressing.
4. Pour dressing over salad and toss until lightly coated.

# Mac'n'Cheese Bake

Please note: Noodles in the solar oven do not cook the same way nor do they taste the same way as noodles boiled on the stove.

## INGREDIENTS:

- 16 ounce. box of macaroni noodles, uncooked
- 1-13 ounce can of evaporated milk
- 1/2 cup butter
- 2 cups milk
- 1-4 ounce can of diced chilies
- 8 ounces of Velveeta cheese
- 1 teaspoon salt
- 1/2 Tablespoon pepper

DIRECTIONS:

1. Set up solar oven.
2. In a large bowl, stir together all ingredients.
3. Add to solar oven pans – divide equally between the two.
4. Add pan with lid to solar oven and seal.
5. Let cook for 4-6 hours.

## Traditional
## Mac'n'Cheese

You can also make this recipe with pre-cooked noodles. And use your solar oven as a way to melt your cheese. Reduce milk to 1 cup add al dente cooked noodles. Reduce time to 2 hours, stirring every 30 minutes.

# Roasted Garlic

INGREDIENTS:
- 1-2 large cloves of garlic
- Aluminum foil

DIRECTIONS:
1. Set up solar oven.
2. Cut the tops of the garlic off so that you can see each of the cloves.
3. Wrap each garlic clove in foil and seal.
4. Add to solar oven pan.
5. Add pan with lid to solar oven and seal.
6. Let cook for 4-6 hours or until garlic is soft and creamy.

Serve as a spread on bread or meat. You can also eat direct from the clove.

# Baked Radish & Turnips

## INGREDIENTS:

- 1 bundle of radishes, washed and sliced thin
- 3 small to medium purple top turnips (or your favorite type of turnips), washed and sliced thin
- 1 teaspoon garlic powder
- 1 teaspoon Italian seasoning – page 186
- 2 Tablespoons olive oil or coconut oil

## DIRECTIONS:

1. Set up solar oven.
2. Cut the tops of the garlic off so that you can see each of the cloves.
3. Wrap each garlic clove in foil and seal.
4. Add to solar oven pan.
5. Add pan with lid to solar oven and seal.
6. Let cook for 4-6 hours.

# Garlic Endives

## INGREDIENTS:

- 3 endives, cut in half, longways
- 4 Tablespoons butter, melted
- 3 cloves of garlic, pressed or minced

## DIRECTIONS:

1. Set up solar oven.
2. Place cut endives in solar oven pan, cut side facing up.
3. In a separate bowl, mix together garlic and butter.
4. Pour butter mixture over the endives.
5. Add pan with lid to solar oven and seal.
6. Let cook for 2 hours.

# Add your Own Favorite Side Dish

Title: _____

## INGREDIENTS:

_____     _____
_____     _____
_____     _____
_____     _____
_____     _____
_____     _____
_____     _____

## DIRECTIONS:

_____
_____
_____
_____
_____
_____
_____
_____
_____
_____

# Add your Own Favorite Side Dish

Title: _____

## INGREDIENTS:

_____    _____
_____    _____
_____    _____
_____    _____
_____    _____
_____    _____

## DIRECTIONS:

_____
_____
_____
_____
_____
_____
_____
_____
_____
_____

# Add your Own Favorite Side Dish

Title: _____

## INGREDIENTS:

_____    _____
_____    _____
_____    _____
_____    _____
_____    _____
_____    _____
_____    _____

## DIRECTIONS:

_____
_____
_____
_____
_____
_____
_____
_____
_____
_____

Larry and I took our solar oven to a Cub Scout overnight camp in the fall of 2013. Elwyn and I had a roast with potatoes and carrots in the oven all day. I can't count how many people stopped to both smell our yummy concoction and to ask about our ovens and how they worked... I was honored to know that all 3 of my boy and cub scouts could answer questions.

# GOING MEATLESS

I have to admit, this family LOVES meat. In all honestly, these kids are a bunch of carnivores! But we do have a few dishes that are meat free. (And if you ask Griffen, he will serve them with a side of beef!)

- Ratatouille
- Cheese Stuffed Mushrooms
- Southwest Stuffed Bell Peppers
- Beans only Chili
- Hummus
    - Sun Dried Tomato Hummus
    - Red Pepper Hummus
    - Spinach Herb Hummus
    - Creamy Greek Yogurt Hummus
    - Avacado Hummus Dip
    - Green Goddess Fresh Herb Hummus
- Zucchini Pizza

# Ratatouille

## INGREDIENTS:

- 2 large onions, sliced
- 1 large eggplant, peeled and sliced
- 4 small zucchini, sliced
- 1 red bell pepper, seeded & cut in thin strips
- 1 green bell pepper, seeded & cut in thin strips
- 6 large tomato; cut in 1/2" wedges
- 1 t fresh basil (or 1-1/2 dried basil)
- 2 t salt
- 1/2 t pepper
- 2 garlic cloves; pressed or minced
- 1 T fresh or dried oregano
- 1T  fresh parsley; chopped
- 1/4 cup olive oil

## DIRECTIONS:

1. Layer half the vegetables in the solar oven pot in the following order: onion, eggplant, zucchini, garlic, green peppers and tomatoes. Then repeat.
2. Sprinkle basil, salt, pepper, and parsley over top.
3. Drizzle with olive oil.
4. Add pan to solar oven and seal.

5. Let cook all day in oven.

This is a late summer favorite in our house when we have a ton of left over zucchinis and egg plants from our garden.

We do grow every ingredient in our garden every year.

# Cheesy Stuffed Mushrooms

## INGREDIENTS:

- 15 large baby bellas mushrooms, remove stems and leave caps intact
- 1/3 cup feta cheese
- 2 Tablespoons  olive oil
- 1 Tablespoon Italian season – page 186

## DIRECTIONS:

1. Set up solar oven.
2. Fill each mushroom cap with cheese and place in solar oven pan.
3. Drizzle oil across the caps.
4. Sprinkle with Italian seasoning.
5. Add to solar oven pan.
6. Add pan with lid to solar oven and seal.
7. Let cook for 2-3 hours.

# Southwest Stuffed Bell Peppers

## INGREDIENTS:

- 4 large bell peppers
- 1 can black beans, drained and rinsed
- 1/2 cup frozen corn
- 1 cup salsa
- 1/2 cup red onion
- 1 can diced green chilies or 2 whole chilies diced
- 1/2 cup rice, uncooked
- 1 cup shredded cheddar cheese
- 1 tsp chili powder – page 90
- 2 Tablespoon cilantro chopped

## DIRECTIONS:

1. Set up solar oven.
2. Cut the tops off of the bell peppers.
3. In a bowl mix remaining ingredients.
4. Divide the mixture and fill each bell pepper.
5. Place filled peppers in solar oven pan.
6. Add pan with lid to solar oven and seal.
7. Let cook for 6 hours in oven or until cooked completely through.

# "Beans Only" Chili

## INGREDIENTS:

- 1/2 cup chopped onion
- 2 cloves garlic, pressed or minced
- 1 green bell pepper, chopped
- 1-4 ounce
- 1 28-ounce can of crushed tomatoes
- 1-8 ounce can of tomato sauce
- 3 cups dried pinto beans
- 1 teaspoon salt
- 1 teaspoon freshly ground black pepper
- 1 tablespoon chili powder – page 90
- 3 cups water

## DIRECTIONS:

**Soak beans overnight in water.**

1. Set up solar oven.
2. Rinse soaked beans and put into solar oven pan.
3. Add all ingredients into solar oven pan and stir well.
4. Add pan with lid to solar oven and seal.
5. Let cook for 4-6 hours or until garlic is soft and creamy.

# Hummus

## INGREDIENTS:

- 2 cups dried chick peas
- 4 cups water

Directions:

Soak chickpeas overnight in water.

1. Set up solar oven
2. Rinse soaked beans and put into solar oven pan, adding the 4 cups of water.
3. Add all ingredients into solar oven pan and stir well.
4. Add pan with lid to solar oven and seal.
5. Let cook for 6-8 hours or until chickpeas are soft.

Once chickpeas are cooked, follow one of the following recipes to make a fantastic and delicious dip or spread.

# Sun Dried Tomato

# Hummus

**INGREDIENTS**:

- 2 cups of cooked chickpeas
- 2 Tablespoon extra virgin olive oil
- 1 garlic cloves
- 3 Tablespoon sun dried tomatoes in oil
- 2 Tablespoon parsley
- 2 Tablespoon of Lemon Juice
- 1/2 - 1 cup water to get desired consistency

Tahini is a "butter" made from hulled, ground sesame seeds.

Puree all ingredients in a food processor and blend until smooth. Add additional water to get desired consistency.

Serve with fresh pita, pita chips, sliced vegetables or whole grain crackers.

# Red Pepper Hummus

Ingredients:

- 2 cups of cooked chickpeas
- 1/2 teaspoon pepper
- 1/2 teaspoon salt
- 1-1/2 Tablespoon extra virgin olive oil
- 3 garlic cloves, pressed or minced
- 3 Tablespoon Tahini
- Splash of Lemon Juice
- 1/2 cup roasted red peppers
- 1/2 - 1 cup water to get desired consistency

Puree all ingredients in a food processor and blend until smooth. Add additional water to get desired consistency.

Serve with fresh pita, pita chips, sliced vegetables or whole grain crackers.

# Spinach Herb Hummus

Ingredients:

- 2 cups of cooked chickpeas
- 1 Tablespoon Extra Virgin Olive Oil
- 3 garlic cloves
- 1 8 ounce block of cream cheese
- 1 Tablespoon tahini
- Splash of Lemon Juice
- 2 cups fresh spinach (you can also use 1 cup of frozen spinach, thawed)
- 1 tablespoon Italian seasonings – page 186
- 1 Tablespoon fresh basil
- 1/2 teaspoon pepper
- 1/2 teaspoon salt
- 1/2 - 1 cup water to get desired consistency

Puree all ingredients in a food processor and blend until smooth. Add additional water if needed to get desired consistency.

Serve with fresh pita, pita chips, sliced vegetables or whole grain crackers.

# Creamy Greek Yogurt

# Hummus

Ingredients:

- 2 cups of cooked chickpeas
- 1 Tablespoon extra virgin olive oil
- 3 garlic cloves
- 1/2 cup plain yogurt
- 1 Tablespoon tahini
- Splash of lemon juice
- 1/2 teaspoon pepper
- 1/2 teaspoon salt
- 1/2 - 1 cup water to get desired consistency

Puree all ingredients in a food processor and blend until smooth. Add additional water if needed to get desired consistency.

Serve with fresh pita, pita chips, sliced vegetables or whole grain crackers.

# Avocado-Hummus

Ingredients:

- 2 medium Hass avocados, peeled and chopped
- 2 cups of cooked chickpeas
- 1/4 cup fresh lemon juice
- 1-1/2 tablespoons tahini
- 1/2 cup extra-virgin olive oil, plus more for drizzling
- 1/2 teaspoon pepper
- 1/2 teaspoon salt
- 1/2 - 1 cup water to get desired consistency

Puree all ingredients in a food processor and blend until smooth. Add additional water if needed to get desired consistency.

Serve with fresh pita, pita chips, sliced vegetables or whole grain crackers.

# Green Goddess Fresh Herb

# Hummus

Ingredients:
- 2 cups of cooked chickpeas
- 1 clove garlic, roughly chopped
- 2 tablespoons tahini
- the juice of one small lemon
- extra virgin olive oil
- 1/2 cup water
- 1 heaping cup fresh herbs, roughly chopped (Dill, Basil, Tarragon, and Chives, Thyme, Cilantro, Parsley – or any fresh herbs that you like!!)
- 1/2 teaspoon pepper
- 1/2 teaspoon salt
- 1/2 - 1 cup water to get desired consistency

Puree all ingredients in a food processor and blend until smooth. Add additional water if needed to get desired consistency.

Serve with fresh pita, pita chips, sliced vegetables or whole grain crackers.

# Zucchini Pizza

## INGREDIENTS:

- 2 large Zucchinis, washed and cut long ways
- 1/3 cup marinara sauce – page 81
- 1/4 cup mozzarella cheese, grated
- 1 teaspoon Italian seasoning – page 186
- Garlic salt to taste
- Aluminum foil

## TOPPINGS TO TASTE:

Sliced mushrooms, red onions, bell peppers, dried tomatoes, feta cheese. (If you want, you can add pepperoni, ground beef or sausage,)

## DIRECTIONS:

Soak beans overnight in water.

1. Set up solar oven.
2. Lay out aluminum foil square on table.
3. Place zucchini in center.
4. Layer sauce and cheese on the zucchini.
5. Add preferred toppings on top of "pizza".
6. Sprinkle with Garlic salt and Italian seasonings.
7. Pull up the aluminum foil corners and form a "tent" Do NOT crush the foil down on the top of the zucchini or the toppings will stick.
8. Add pan with lid to solar oven and seal solar oven.
9. Let cook for 1-2 hours or until the zucchini is tender and cheese is melted.

# Add your Own Favorite Meatless Dish

Title: _____

## INGREDIENTS:

_____    _____
_____    _____
_____    _____
_____    _____
_____    _____
_____    _____
_____    _____

## DIRECTIONS:

_____
_____
_____
_____
_____
_____
_____
_____
_____

# Add your Own Favorite Meatless Dish

Title: _____

## INGREDIENTS:

_____    _____
_____    _____
_____    _____
_____    _____
_____    _____
_____    _____
_____    _____

## DIRECTIONS:

_____
_____
_____
_____
_____
_____
_____
_____

# Add your Own Favorite Meatless Dish

Title: _____

**INGREDIENTS:**

_____    _____
_____    _____
_____    _____
_____    _____
_____    _____
_____    _____

**DIRECTIONS:**

_____
_____
_____
_____
_____
_____
_____
_____
_____

# SOUPS

- Chili
- Basic Beef Stew
- Chickpea Chili
- Tuscan Chicken Soup
- Potato Corn Chowder
- Vegetable Soup
- Chicken Tortilla

# Chili

## INGREDIENTS:

- 2 cups dried pinto beans
- 1 pound lean ground beef, uncooked
- 1/2 cup chopped onion
- 2 cloves garlic, pressed or minced
- 1 green bell pepper, chopped
- 1-4 ounce can of diced chilies
- 1 28-ounce can of crushed tomatoes
- 1-8 ounce can of tomato sauce
- 1 teaspoon salt
- 1 teaspoon freshly ground black pepper
- 1 tablespoon chili powder – page 90
- 4 cups water

## DIRECTIONS:

Soak beans overnight in water.

1. Set up solar oven.
2. Crumple meat into separate bowl.
3. Add dried beans and all other ingredients to meat and stir well.
4. Divide the chili into the 2 solar oven pans.
5. Add pans with lids to solar oven and seal.
6. Let cook for 8-10 hours or until beans are soft and meat is cooked through.

# Basic Beef Stew

## INGREDIENTS:

- Beef cut into bite sized cubes (I use the marked down London broil from my local store – you know the last date meat that I throw in the freezer specifically for soups and stews)
- 4 large carrots, chopped into 1/2 inch slices
- 4 large potatoes or 8 small red potatoes, sliced
- 1 cup thinly sliced celery
- 3 gloves of garlic, pressed or minced
- 1/2  red onion chopped
- 6-8 cups water
- 1 Tablespoon of fresh rosemary
- 1 Tablespoon of fresh oregano
- salt and pepper to taste
- optional: 1 can of peas or 1 cup of frozen peas (I use 1 cup of freeze dried peas)

## DIRECTIONS:

1. Set up solar oven.
2. Add all ingredients to a solar oven pots, and stir well.
3. Add pan to solar oven and seal.
4. Let cook 8 -10 hours in solar oven or until meat is cooked.

# Chickpea Chili

Ingredients:
- 1 cup dried chickpeas
- 1 onion chopped
- 5 garlic cloves, pressed or minced
- 1 teaspoon ground cumin
- 1 teaspoon salt
- 1/2 teaspoon ground chili powder – page 90
- 3/4 teaspoon ground cinnamon
- 1/2 teaspoon ground turmeric
- 3 cups chicken broth
- 1 cup water
- 1/2 cup golden raisins
- 1-28-ounce can crushed tomatoes, undrained
- 1 medium butternut squash peeled and chopped.
- 1 cup frozen green peas, thawed
- 2/3 cup sliced pimiento-stuffed olives
- 1/4 cup chopped fresh cilantro

# DIRECTIONS:

**Soak chickpeas overnight in water.**

1. Set up solar oven.
2. Drain chickpeas and add to large separate bowl.
3. Add all other ingredients to bowl and stir well.
4. Divide soup between the 2 solar oven pans equally.
5. Add pans with lids to solar oven and seal.
6. Let cook for 8-10 hours or until chickpeas are soft.

# Tuscan Chicken Soup

INGREDIENTS:

- 1 cup white beans, dried
- 1 cup water
- 1 whole onion, chopped
- 2 Tablespoons tomato paste
- 1/2 teaspoon freshly ground black pepper
- 1/4 teaspoon salt
- 1-14 ounce can chicken broth
- 1 bell pepper, chopped
- 1 pound boneless, skinless chicken breasts or thighs, cut into bite sized pieces
- 3 garlic cloves, pressed or minced
- 1/2 teaspoon chopped fresh rosemary
- 4 cups of fresh baby spinach (or a 6 ounce bag)

## TOPPING

- ¼ cup grated fresh Parmesan cheese

## DIRECTIONS:

Soak beans overnight in water.

1. Set up solar oven
2. Drain beans and add to large separate bowl.
3. Add all other ingredients and stir well.
4. Divide soup between the 2 solar oven pans equally.
5. Add pans with lids to solar oven and seal.
6. Let cook for 8-10 hours or until chickpeas are soft.

# Potato Corn Chowder

- 1-32 ounce package of hash browns
- 1-15 ounce can of creamed corn
- 1-15 ounce can of corn
- 1-12 ounce can of evaporative milk
- 1-14 ounce can of vegetable broth
- 1 bell pepper, chopped into small pieces,
- 1/2 cup onion, chopped
- 2 cloves of garlic, pressed or minced
- 1/2 cup celery, chopped
- 1/2 cup carrots, grated
- 1 teaspoon black pepper
- 1 teaspoon salt

DIRECTIONS:

1. Set up solar oven.
2. Add all ingredients to a solar oven pots and stir together until well blended.
3. Add pan to solar oven and seal.
4. Let cook 6-8 hours in oven.

# Vegetable Soup

## INGREDIENTS:

- 1 large onion, chopped
- 4 garlic cloves, pressed or minced
- 2 large carrots, chopped
- 2 small celery ribs, chopped
- 1 medium turnip, chopped
- 1 green bell pepper, chopped
- 3 green onions, sliced thin
- 1/2 cup snow peas in pods or ½ cup frozen peas
- 6 cups chicken broth (or vegetable broth)
- 1/2 teaspoon thyme
- 1 teaspoon ground black pepper
- 1/2 teaspoon salt

## DIRECTIONS:

1. Set up solar oven.
2. In a large bowl, mix together all ingredients.
3. Divide soup between the 2 solar oven pans equally.
4. Add pans with lids to solar oven and seal.
5. Let cook for 8-10 hours or until vegetables are soft.

# Chicken Tortilla Soup

## INGREDIENTS:

- 1lb chicken breast, trimmed and sliced into small 1/4 inch chunks
- 1-15 ounce can sweet whole corn kernels, drained
- 1-15 ounce can diced tomatoes, drained
- 1 medium onion, chopped
- 3/4 cup green pepper, chopped
- 1 jalapeno pepper, minced
- 2 cloves garlic, pressed or minced
- 1/4 cup cilantro chopped, fine
- 1/4 cup green onions, sliced
- 1/4 teaspoon chili powder – page 90
- 1 teaspoon salt
- 1 teaspoon ground pepper
- 5 cups chicken stock

## TOPPING:

- Monterey Jack cheese, shredded, sliced avocado, and sliced corn tortillas or tortilla chips.

## DIRECTIONS:

1. Set up solar oven.
2. In a large bowl, mix together all ingredient, except for the cheese for the topping.
3. Divide soup between the 2 solar oven pans equally.
4. Add pans with lids to solar oven and seal.
5. Let cook for 8-10 hours or until vegetables are soft.

When serving, sprinkle cheese on top and add several tortilla chips and a slice or 2 of avocado.

# Add your Own Favorite Soup

Title: _____

## INGREDIENTS:

_____    _____
_____    _____
_____    _____
_____    _____
_____    _____
_____    _____
_____    _____

## DIRECTIONS:

_____
_____
_____
_____
_____
_____
_____
_____
_____

# Add your Own Favorite Soup

Title: _____

## INGREDIENTS:

_____    _____
_____    _____
_____    _____
_____    _____
_____    _____
_____    _____
_____    _____

## DIRECTIONS:

_____
_____
_____
_____
_____
_____
_____
_____
_____

# Add your Own Favorite Soup

Title: _____

INGREDIENTS:

_____    _____
_____    _____
_____    _____
_____    _____
_____    _____
_____    _____

DIRECTIONS:

_____
_____
_____
_____
_____
_____
_____
_____

# BREADS, BAKED GOODS AND DESSERTS

- Cornbread
- Everyday Sandwich Bread
- Biscuits
- Dump Cake
  - Yellow cake mix
- Oatmeal Coconut Cake
- Baked Apples
- Banana Brownies
- Chocolate Chip Zucchini Bread
- Chess Squares
- Baked Banana
- S'mores

# SOLAR OVEN BAKING TIPS AND TRICKS

Did you know that you can make cookies in your solar oven? Take your favorite cookie recipe and mix together as normal (or use your favourite refrigerator cookie dough).

Flip your pans over in your solar oven and use the bottoms of the pans as cookie sheets. On a warm day with full sun, you can cook a batch of cookies in about 60 minutes!!

# Baked Apples

## INGREDIENTS:

- 6 large apples, washed and sliced
- 4 Tablespoons butter, melted
- 1 Tablespoon ground cinnamon
- 1 teaspoon ground nutmeg

## DIRECTIONS:

1. Set up solar oven.
2. In solar oven pan, layer apples.
3. Pour butter over the apple and sprinkle with cinnamon and nutmeg.
4. Add pan with lid to solar oven and seal.
5. Let cook for 4-6 hours.

# Solar Cookin' Cornbread

## INGREDIENTS:

- 1/4 cup flour
- 3/4 cup cornmeal
- 1/4 cup sugar
- 4 teaspoons baking powder
- 1 teaspoon salt
- 1 egg
- 1 1/4 cup milk
- 1/3 cup melted butter
- 1 can sweet corn kernels
- 1-4 ounce can of green chilies

## DIRECTIONS:

1. Set up solar oven.
2. Thoroughly grease the inside of your solar oven pan and set aside.
3. Mix the dry ingredients together in a bowl.
4. Mix in the wet ingredients until blended.
5. Pour into the greased solar oven pan.
6. Add pan with lid to solar oven and seal.
7. Let cook for 6+ hours.

# Everyday Bread

## INGREDIENTS:

- 3-1/4 cups flour
- 1-1/2 cups lukewarm water
- 3/4 Tablespoon yeast
- 3/4 Tablespoons kosher or Celtic salt

## DIRECTIONS:

1. Set up solar oven.
2. Mix together warm water, yeast and salt in a large bowl. Let set 3-4 minutes.
3. Stir in flour. (We use our kitchen aid for this with the dough hook attachment.)
4. Allow dough to rise for 2+ hours. – We normally make our bread dough the night before and start with step 5 first thing in the morning so that we have fresh bread for dinner the next night)
5. Grease solar oven pans. Once the dough has had time to rise, divide into 2 equal parts and form a shaped loaf.
6. Add loaves to 2 round solar oven pans and let rise for 45 more minutes.
7. Place in solar oven pan and let bake all day We normally cook it for 8+ hours. Remember that your bread will NOT get a "crisp brown top".

Optional: during step 5 add Italian season – page 186, Onion seasoning – page 188 or cheddar cheese to make a flavored bread.

# Buttermilk Biscuits

INGREDIENTS:

- 2 cups all-purpose flour
- 2 teaspoons baking powder
- 1/4 teaspoon baking soda
- 1 teaspoon salt
- 7 tablespoons unsalted butter, cut into thin slices, chilled in freezer
- 3/4 cup cold buttermilk

You can also add cheese or other seasonings to the dough to make a flavored biscuit for dinner. Our sprinkle the top with garlic salt for something tasty!

## Directions:

1. Set up solar oven and grease solar oven pans.
2. Whisk flour, baking powder, salt, and baking soda together in a large bowl.
3. Cut butter into flour mixture with a pastry blender until the mixture resembles coarse crumbs.
4. Make a well in the center of butter and flour mixture. Pour in 3/4 cup buttermilk; stir until just combined.
5. Turn dough onto a floured work surface, pat together into a rectangle.
6. Fold dough 3 times and then roll dough on a floured surface to about 1/2 inch thick.
7. Cut out 12 biscuits using a 2 1/2-inch round biscuit cutter.
8. Add biscuits to the solar oven pans. Edges of biscuits can touch each other.
9. Add pan with lid to solar oven and seal.
10. Let cook for 3+ hours or until biscuits are cooked through.

# Dump Cake

## INGREDIENTS:

- 2 cans of sliced peaches, raspberries or pears, including juice or 3 cups fresh plus 1/2 cup water.
- 1 box of cake mix – or use the recipe on page 171. We have made this with a gluten-free cake mix.
- 4 Tablespoons butter, divided into 8 pieces
- 1/4 cup brown sugar

## DIRECTIONS:

1. Set up solar oven.
2. In a large bowl, mix together cans of fruit and cake mix (you do NOT need to add the ingredients listed on the cake box).
3. Pour into solar oven pan.
4. Sprinkle brown sugar evenly on top of cake batter.
5. Place all 8 pieces around the top of the batter.
6. Add pan with lid to solar oven and seal.
7. Let cook for 6+ hours.

Serve with Ice Cream.

In our house, we don't use boxed cake mix. Rather, we make all of our foods from scratch. Here is our yellow cake mix recipe.

## Yellow Cake Mix

*Homemade box cake mix*
- 2-1/4 cups all purpose flour
- 1-1/2 cups sugar
- 1/3 cups dry instant milk powder
- 1 teaspoons salt
- 1 Tablespoon baking powder

*To create your cake, Add the following ingredients to Cake Mix above.*
- 1 teaspoon vanilla
- ½ cup softened butter
- 3 eggs
- 1-1/4 cups water

Preheat oven to 350°. Beat all ingredients together with an electric mixer for 3 minutes or until well blended and pour into a greased 9x13 pan. . Bake for 25-30 minutes or until an inserted toothpick comes out clean.

# Oatmeal Coconut Cake

## INGREDIENTS & DIRECTIONS:

### Oatmeal Cake Recipe
1. Set up solar oven pan.
2. Pour 2 cups boiling water over 1 cup old-fashioned oatmeal. Let cool.
3. Mix together:
    - 1 cup brown sugar
    - 1 cup white sugar
    - 1/2 cup Butter
    - 2 eggs
    - 1-1/2 cups flour
    - 1 teaspoon baking soda
    - 1/2 teaspoon cinnamon
    - 1/4 cup shredded coconut
    - Pinch of Salt
4. Add cooled oatmeal and mix well.
5. Place batter in solar oven pan.

## OATMEAL CAKE TOPPING

6. In a separate bowl, mix together the following ingredients:
   - 1 cup brown sugar
   - 1/2 cup walnuts
   - 1/2 cup coconut
   - 1 teaspoon vanilla
   - 6 Tablespoons melted butter
   - 1/4 cup milk

7. Put topping on warm Oatmeal Cake batter in the solar oven pan.

8. Add pan with lid to solar oven and seal.

9. Let cook for 6+ hours.

# Banana Brownies

- 1-1/2 cup sugar
- 1cup sour cream
- 1/2 cup butter, softened
- 2 eggs
- 4 ripe bananas, mashed
- 2 teaspoon vanilla extract
- 2 cup all purpose flour
- 1 teaspoon baking soda
- 3/4 teaspoon salt
- 1/2 cup chopped walnuts (optional)

Brown Butter Frosting:

- 1/2 cup butter, melted
- 4 cups powdered sugar
- 2 teaspoon vanilla extract
- 3 teaspoons milk

## DIRECTIONS:

1. Set up solar oven
2. Grease solar oven pan.
3. In a separate bowl, beat together sugar, sour cream, butter, and eggs until creamy.
4. Blend in bananas and vanilla extract.
5. Add flour, baking soda, and salt.
6. Stir in walnuts.
7. Spread batter evenly into pan. Bake in solar oven for 90 minutes or until "set".

## FOR FROSTING:

8. Stir together melted butter, powdered sugar, vanilla extract and milk. Whisk together until smooth
9. Spread the butter frosting over the warm bars. Cut and serve.

# Chocolate Chip Zucchini Bread

## INGREDIENTS:

- 2 large eggs
- 1/3 cup honey
- 1/2 cup vegetable oil
- 1/2 cup brown sugar, packed
- 1 teaspoon vanilla extract
- 1 teaspoon salt
- 1/2 teaspoon baking soda
- 1/2 teaspoon baking powder
- 1/3 cup cocoa powder
- 2 cups all-purpose flour
- 2 cups shredded zucchini
- 1 cup chocolate chips

## DIRECTIONS:

1. Set up solar oven.
2. In a large mixing bowl, beat the eggs, honey, oil, sugar, and vanilla until smooth.
3. Add the salt, baking soda, baking powder, cocoa, and flour. Mix well.
4. Stir in the zucchini and chocolate chips. Pour the batter into your solar oven pan.
5. Add pan with lid to solar oven and seal.
6. Let cook for 4-6 hours.

# Chess Squares

My grandmother made these years ago! She would add a little lemon zest into the top layer to give it a citrus flair.

## INGREDIENTS:

- 2-1/4 cups all purpose flour
- 1-1/2 cups sugar
- 1/3 cups dry instant milk powder
- 1 teaspoons salt
- 1 Tablespoon baking powder
- 3 eggs
- 8 oz cream cheese, softened
- 1/2 cup butter, melted
- 4 cups powdered sugar

## DIRECTIONS:

1. Set up solar oven.
2. Mix flour, sugar, milk powder, salt, baking powder, melted butter and one egg together.
3. . Press into the bottom of the solar oven pan.
4. Then in a separate bowl, mix the powdered sugar, softened cream cheese and two eggs until smooth.
5. Spread on top of 1st layer.
6. Add pan with lid to solar oven and seal.
7. Let cook for 4 hour or dessert is cooked through.

# Baked Bananas

This is an aluminum foil recipe which is for a single serving recipe. We make these 10 at a time in our house.

## INGREDIENTS:

- 1 banana; peeled and sliced in half longways.
- 1/4 cup chocolate chips
- 1/4 cup mini marshmallows
- 1/2 teaspoon cinnamon
- Aluminum foil

## DIRECTIONS:

1. Set up solar oven.
2. Lay a square of foil down and place your peeled banana in the middle.
3. Sprinkle your chocolate and mini marshmallows in between the two halves.
4. Sprinkle on your cinnamon.
5. Pull the corners of the foil up to form a "tent" and twist to make a sealed foil pocket. Do not wrap tightly because your marshmallows will stick to the top.
6. Add each banana tent to solar oven and seal oven.
7. Let cook for 30 minutes until mini marshmallows and chocolate is melted.

# Baked S'mores

## INGREDIENTS:

- 2 cups of crushed graham crackers
- 1 cup butter melted
- 1/2 cup sugar
- 1-1/2 cups chocolate chips, semi-sweet
- 1 cup of mini marshmallows

## DIRECTIONS:

1. Set up solar oven.
2. Mix together graham crackers, butter and sugar until well blended.
3. Grease pan.
4. Press the "dough" into the bottom and up the sides of a solar oven pan.
5. Sprinkle on chocolate chips and marshmallows.
6. Add pan with lid to solar oven and seal.
7. Let cook for 1 hour or until chocolate and marshmallows are melted.

# Add your Own Favorite Dessert or Baked Good

Title: _____

INGREDIENTS:

_____    _____
_____    _____
_____    _____
_____    _____
_____    _____
_____    _____

DIRECTIONS:

_____
_____
_____
_____
_____
_____
_____
_____
_____

# Add your Own Favorite Dessert or Baked Good

Title: _____

## INGREDIENTS:

| | |
|---|---|
| _____ | _____ |
| _____ | _____ |
| _____ | _____ |
| _____ | _____ |
| _____ | _____ |
| _____ | _____ |

## DIRECTIONS:

_____

_____

_____

_____

_____

_____

_____

_____

_____

# Add your Own Favorite Dessert or Baked Good

Title: _____

INGREDIENTS:

_____  _____
_____  _____
_____  _____
_____  _____
_____  _____
_____  _____

DIRECTIONS:

_____
_____
_____
_____
_____
_____
_____
_____
_____
_____

# Add your Own Favorite Dessert or Baked Good

Title: _____

## INGREDIENTS:

_____    _____

_____    _____

_____    _____

_____    _____

_____    _____

_____    _____

## DIRECTIONS:

_____

_____

_____

_____

_____

_____

_____

_____

_____

# EXTRAS

- Italian seasonings
- Lemon Pepper Seasonings
- Jen's Onion Soup Spice Mix

# Italian Seasoning

## INGREDIENTS:

- 1/3 cup dried oregano leaves
- 1 tablespoon. garlic powder
- 2 teaspoon. onion salt
- 1/3 cup dried basil leaves
- 1/4 cup dried thyme leaves

## DIRECTIONS FOR MIX:

Mix all ingredients together. Store in an airtight container.

# Lemon Pepper
# Seasoning

## INGREDIENTS:

- 8 large lemons
- 1/2 cup of crushed pepper corns
- 1/4 cup kosher or sea salt

## DIRECTIONS FOR MIX:

1. Zest all the lemons. Mix lemon zest with crushed peppercorns.
2. Spread out on parchment lined baking sheet and bake on lowest setting until the zest is completely dried  or dehydrate in your food dehydrator.
3. Add the lemon-pepper to a food processor and grind until desired texture.
4. Mix with the kosher salt and store in an airtight container.

# Jen's Onion Soup Spice

## INGREDIENTS:

- 1/2 cup Dehydrated onion flakes
- 2 Tablespoons Onion Powder
- 1 Tablespoon Garlic Granules
- 1 teaspoon Celery seeds
- 1/2 teaspoon Ground Pepper
- 1 Tablespoon Celtic sea salt

## DIRECTIONS FOR MIX:

Mix all ingredients together. Store in an airtight container.

# CREATING YOUR OWN SOLAR OVEN

There are many, many different types of solar oven designs out there. You can create one with simple supplies such as a silver car shade or 2 cardboard boxes and some aluminum foil. Although we have purchased our two, I have some very inventive boys in our household.

Building a solar oven is not complicated. (Hey, my 12 year old son, Griffen has been making these for FUN to use to heat up his lunches! I guess that's what we get for having 4 boy scouts and cub scouts in our home.)

Start by gathering your supplies. You will need the following:

- **3 cardboard boxes** They need to be about to fit inside each other to "nest" inside each other. The 2 largest need to be fairly close in size.
- **1 roll of aluminum foil**
- **Insulation** for in the middle of your 2 boxes. Shredded or rolled newspaper works great! We had a roll of butcher paper that we tore pieces off and crumpled.
- **Piece of Plexiglas**, sheet of clingfilm, or ziplock bag (We found Oven bags for Turkeys at our local grocery store in the aluminum foil section.
- **Ruler**
- **DuctTape**
- **Box Cutter & Scissors**
- **A stick or dowel rod** to use as an opener. A metal hanger would work as well.

## DIRECTIONS:

1. Fold the flaps in on your medium box and duct tape them down.

2. The smallest box needs to be even in height with the medium box... so cut it down if needed.

3. Line the smallest box with aluminum foil. Tape edges down.

4. Insert the smallest box into the largest box. There should be a inch or 2 in between the boxes.

For best results, use a dark colored pan with a lid that fits inside the smallest box and add a thermometer inside so that you can monitor the temperature. If you cannot see the thermometer, do not keep opening up the oven. It will let out all of your hot air!

5. Add insulation around the outside of the smallest box, inside the medium. This will also allow the smallest box to stay stable inside the medium box.

6. Now, for the "lid". The largest box needs to have a fairly tight fit on the medium box. Cut off the flaps of the box and tape the edges. The box will be placed upside down over the medium box to create a lid.

7. With your box cutter, create a "flap" in the bottom of the box. This will serve as your reflector. You will need to cut one long edge and 2 short edges, leaving at least 2 inches to the edge of the box.

8. Flip the lid over. On the inside, you will need to tape down your cling film or plexiglas. We used an oven bag and cut it to fit the inside of the box and tape it secure. This is the seal to keep the light coming into the oven and to keep the heat from escaping.

9. Line the flap with aluminum foil to create a reflector. Secure with duct tape.

10.    Lastly, using a stick or a piece of wire, secure the flap opened up to cause a reflection of sunlight into the oven. This will bounce light around to hit the pan of food. Griffen always duct tapes his stick on so that it doesn't fall.

You can create a solar oven out of wood as well.

# INDEX

# REFERENCES

Kris' Personal Blog for recipes, kids activities, essential oils and crafts:

www.KrisAndLarry.com

---

## Solar Oven and other recipes

Kris' Sister, Jen:

www.TurningCrunchy.com

**Solar Oven Society:**

www.solarovens.org/recipes/

We carry solar ovens online at

**www.mazys.com**

# BOOKS BY KRIS MAZY

You can find all of Kris Mazy's books online at

## www.MazyBooks.com

**A KITCHEN FULL OF MIXES –**   So many people have allergies to the processed food that are out there on the market. In this book, Kris Mazy, mom of 5 kids plus 2 (including 1 autistic and 1 with severe allergies to dyes) shows simple recipes that you can make in your kitchen that are dye-free, many of which are like grabbing a "box-mix" from the grocery store.

(release date: September 2012)

**COOKING WITH MAMA** – Kids learn to bake cookies – Kris introduces cooking to kids in this Children's book about a little girl named Reagan.
(release date: May 2013)

**AN OUTDOOR KITCHEN FULL OF SUNSHINE** – Using a solar oven, you can cook almost anything and save on your power bill by using the sun. This book contains everyday recipes that you can cook using a solar oven. (release date: June 2014)

Kris' personal blog of recipes, homeschooling and crafts is located at **www.krisandlarry.com**

# ABOUT THE AUTHOR

Kris grew up in the mountains of Arizona and is married with 7 children, Shelby, Griffen, Elwyn, Berlyn, Rowan, Breckin and Trystan along with occasional foster children. She and her husband, Larry (photo above) love playing outside, geocaching and spending time it the garden. Kris is very close with her family, living next door to her parents and down the road to her brother-in-law, sister and their children. Their garden consists of tomatoes, eggplant, onions, peppers, peas, green beans, zucchini, squashes and more along with an intensive herb garden and "berry walk" that is added to every year. They enjoy solar cooking and finding new "convenience" recipes to make for their ever changing family.

"Cooking for a larger family can take a bit of extra planning but I love the fact that I can put everything in my solar oven, seal it up and let nature cook dinner for me while I am out being a mom. Cooking from scratch takes no more time that the boxed foods to create and making my own mixes and freezer meals allows me to stay an active mom in my kids' lives."

Kris has Associates of Arts in Fine Arts, Photography, and Bachelors of Science in Education and is working towards a Masters of Arts in Human Services, Marriage and Family Counseling. She has worked not only as a mom, but has her own photo studio and website / graphic design business. In the past, Kris had a line of scrapbook products out on the market, both in print and in digital. Her love of cooking has really pushed sharing recipes with her blog and facebook readers. She also sells and uses essential oils and instructs many different types of classes, including scrapbooking, essential oils and photography.

37055260R00111

Made in the USA
San Bernardino, CA
08 August 2016